THE GRUMPY GUY

NICOLA MARSH

Copyright © Nicola Marsh 2022
Published by Parlance Press 2022

All the characters, names, places and incidents in this book have no existence outside the imagination of the author and have no relation whatsoever to anyone bearing the same name or names and are used fictitiously. They're not distantly inspired by any individual known or unknown to the author and all the incidents in the book are pure invention. Any resemblance to actual events, locales, or persons, living or dead, is coincidental.

All rights reserved including the right of reproduction in any form. The text or any part of the publication may not be reproduced or transmitted in any form without the written permission of the publisher.

The author acknowledges the copyrighted or trademarked status and trademark owners of the word marks mentioned in this work of fiction.

First Published by Harlequin Enterprises in 2010 as WIFE AND MOTHER WANTED, by Nicola Marsh
World English Rights Copyright © 2021 Nicola Marsh

Fairy shop owner Carissa Lewis has a new neighbour and he's grumpy, infuriating, and way too gorgeous. She's determined to keep her distance from the single dad, but Brody's adorable daughter Molly has other ideas.

Brody Elliott is doing it tough raising his young daughter. He harbours guilt for the loss of Molly's mother and will do anything to protect his little girl from heartbreak again. So when Molly befriends their vivacious new neighbour, he's wary.

But what's a guy to do when he can't fight the relentless attraction between him and the lovely Carissa? Does the dour dad have room in his heart for love?

One

"I don't believe this."

Carissa Lewis collapsed into a garden chair and resisted the urge to throw her cell into the nearby pond. Though she wouldn't risk it. The way her luck was running today, she'd probably decapitate Fred, her favourite ceramic frog.

Instead, she took a deep breath, gritted her teeth and lowered her voice. "Peter, how could you do this to me? To the kids? We were counting on you."

Her boyfriend of eight months—eight far too long months—said, "You shouldn't ask so much of people. I've had enough."

She shook her head, wondering if the late nights she'd been keeping in preparation for the annual Easter pageant had melted her brain. How could asking Peter to play the Easter bunny for the local kids in town be asking too much? The guy didn't have a heart, a fact she'd slowly realised over the course of their lukewarm relationship but hadn't got around to doing anything about.

She had a thing for 'comfortable' boyfriends, guys that

didn't challenge her, or make demands, or set off any fireworks in her vicinity. She liked it that way. Comfortable was good and the antithesis of her totally uncomfortable childhood, when she would've given anything for someone to depend on.

She tried a different approach. "This is important to me. Won't you reconsider please?"

"Sorry, babe. I want out. Of everything."

Her heart stilled for all of two seconds before the adrenalin kicked in again. "Are you dumping me? You weak, spineless, son of a—"

The dial tone hummed in her ear and she let out a frustrated yell, leapt to her feet, and jumped up and down on the spot like a two year old having a doozy of a tantrum.

"What are you staring at?" she said to Fred, finding his wide froggy grin smug rather than endearing at that moment. "Where am I going to find an Easter bunny now?"

It had to be the time of year. Things always went wrong at Easter. Her parents had died at Easter when she'd been three, she'd been adopted out a year later to the family from hell, and she always seemed to hang onto some loser like Peter to avoid being alone with her memories around this time.

Yep, Easter stunk and looked like this year was no exception.

"My daddy says to look under the nearest bush," a small, high-pitched voice said from somewhere over her new neighbour's fence, "though everyone knows it's way too early for the Easter bunny to arrive. He's practising his hopping for next week."

Carissa looked up and spied a splash of red in the towering eucalypt's lower branches, the bright material ending above a set of scraped knees covered in a patchwork of sticky bandages.

"You could be right," Carissa said, hoping the pint-sized person to whom those legs belonged knew her way around trees, for she'd hate for the little girl to take a tumble.

She'd heard about her new neighbours who had moved in a week ago. A single father with a girl of about six, and though she'd been meaning to welcome them with a batch of her home-made brownies, she hadn't got around to it yet.

Or maybe it had something to do with the brief glimpse she'd caught of the father as he'd unloaded his car. Long, lean legs and a firm, cute butt in faded denim as he'd bent over the trunk had her taking a second look, a long second look, which had almost culminated in her steering her car onto the lawn rather than up her driveway.

And though she'd barely seen his face when he'd looked up to see what the commotion was about as she'd grazed a trash can while over-correcting, that one illicit ogle at his butt had sent her welcome committee plans up in smoke. She'd been way too embarrassed to face him after he'd witnessed her atrocious parking skills.

"What's your name, sweetheart?" Carissa asked, hoping to talk the little girl out of the tree and put a face to the stubby legs. "Mine's Carissa."

"Molly Jane Elliott." The soft voice pronounced it like a title bestowed by a queen. "But you can call me Molly."

Smiling, Carissa wandered over to the fence and peered into the tree's lower branches, still unable to catch a glimpse of the friendly little girl. "Pleased to meet you, Molly. Would you like to come down and meet Fred? He's my favourite frog but I have loads of others."

Molly hesitated for all of two seconds before scrambling down in a flash of legs and arms, landing in a none-too-gracious heap at the bottom of the tree.

"You okay, sweetie?"

Molly nodded. "Yeah, that's how I always land. I get a sticky bandage every time." She pointed to her knees and grinned, displaying a darling gap where a front tooth should be.

However, Carissa didn't glance at Molly's knees. Instead, she stared at the girl's face in shock, seeing a startling resemblance to herself at that age: messy blonde curls, wary blue eyes and a recalcitrant expression that warned "don't mess with me, I may look little but I've seen plenty."

"You look kinda funny, Carissa." Molly had an adorable lisp courtesy of the missing front tooth and combined with her attitude had Carissa almost scrambling the fence in her haste to pick up the pint-sized dynamo and cradle her in her arms.

"That's because I can't find the Easter bunny, remember?"

Nice save. That's all she needed, for Molly to go running to her dad and telling him about their nutcase neighbour, one who stared at his daughter like she wanted one. Which was totally true, of course. She'd give anything to have a family of her own: loving husband, delightful kids, white picket fence, the works.

Unfortunately, all she had was the fence and that had taken a week of blisters and a cricked neck while she put the darn thing up and painted it herself.

Though one thing was for sure. When she had a family of her own, they would love each other, support each other and be the exact opposite of what she'd faced growing up.

"Oh, yeah, though I already told you, it's too early to look for the Easter bunny." Molly stood and dusted off a red cotton pinafore that had seen better days. "Though you said you had some frogs for me to meet?"

"I sure do, though maybe you should ask your dad before coming over to play?"

Molly shook her head, blonde curls bouncing around her chubby face, defiance in her blue eyes. "Nope. Not asking. He'll just make me go inside like he always does."

Great. Now what should she do? She couldn't encourage the child to leave her backyard without permission but she didn't want to disappoint Molly either. She'd had enough of that emotion growing up and there was something about this child that begged her not to dish out more of the same.

As if on cue, a loud voice bellowed from the rear of the run-down house next door. "Molly Jane. Time for lunch. Inside, now."

No please. No coaxing. No gentle words of love.

Yeah, she knew exactly what that felt like and it still hurt twenty years later.

"Don't want to," Molly yelled back, folding her arms and stamping her foot while Carissa bit back a grin.

Oh yeah, looking at Molly was like taking a step back in time and seeing a mirror image of herself at that age, and her heart went out to the little girl all over again.

The town gossips had said Molly's father was a single dad and she'd assumed that meant he was divorced. From Molly's scruffy appearance and rebellious attitude, Carissa wondered how long since the girl's mother had been around.

Was that why Mr. Elliott had moved here, to get away from an ex?

"Molly, I said now!"

Trying not to grimace at the man's impatient tone, Carissa said, "Molly, why don't you go have your lunch and I'll talk to your dad? Maybe you can come over later and see Fred and his friends?"

Some of the tension eased out of Molly's shoulders. "Really?"

Carissa smiled and nodded, hoping she could talk the ogre into letting his daughter spend some time with a stranger. Not that she intended to be a stranger for long.

"Really. Now run along."

Molly sent her a brief, beatific smile before racing across the yard to her backdoor. "Dad! Dad! Carissa wants to talk to you. She's got loads of frogs and everything! And she's looking for the Easter bunny. And she said I can come over and play with her after my lunch. What's for lunch? Will it take long? I wanna play."

Molly's words spilled out in a rush and Carissa saw a man's shadow bend down to the little girl before she ran inside and the man straightened and stepped out of the doorway.

Carissa's breath hitched as she caught her first front-on glimpse of the ogre.

Tall, lean, fighting machine sprung to mind as the man exited the doorway and loped across the backyard toward her. Tension radiated off him in waves as if he had a surplus of energy coiled tight within, and his body language—folded arms, perpetual frown and compressed lips—read "I'm in a bad mood so lay off."

Never mind that the folded arms displayed a great set of biceps at the edge of his short-sleeved black T-shirt or that the shade of the T heightened his dark, brooding good looks. This guy had "bad attitude" written all over him and she'd dealt with his kind before. Having an abusive father had her chomping at the bit to go toe to toe with Mr. Bad-Ass Elliott.

"Hey there, I'm Carissa Lewis, your neighbour."

He halted about two feet in front of her and the rest of what she'd been about to say died on her lips as she struggled not to gawk. If she thought he looked impressive strolling across the lawn, it had nothing on the man close up.

Sure, the frown was still there and the lips had thinned into further disapproval but those eyes...the colour of melted chocolate, the same colour she happily drooled over every night when she dipped ripe strawberries into the mix of milk and bitter chocolate in her fondue pot, her latest eclectic buy.

Their unique colour was accentuated by the longest set of eyelashes she'd ever seen on a guy, giving him a sexy edge at odds with the crinkle between his brows, the one that looked like a permanent fixture.

"The name's Brody," he snapped. "You shouldn't get my daughter's hopes up like that, saying she can come over and play."

Hating that he had her on the back foot already, she said, "I said she should discuss it with you first and we'd have a chat too. I'd love to have her over."

"But I don't know you." His frown deepened, doing little to detract from his good looks.

Though she had no intention of getting involved with a guy after her latest disaster in the dating stakes, if someone came along who looked like this she'd have a hard time not taking a second glance and thinking about it twice.

Perhaps if she went for guys who weren't so safe, guys who were gorgeous and had danger written all over them, she'd have more luck?

As if. This was real life, not fantasy land, and if anyone should know, she should. Losing her parents in a freak avalanche had landed her in an orphanage where she'd spent a year battling bullies, starvation, and a mouse infestation that left her shuddering at the thought of the little critters to this day. When she'd been adopted out a year later, she'd taken one look at her new parents and all but launched herself into their arms.

However, if the orphanage had been a bad dream, living with the Lovells had been a nightmare. For all their fancy clothes and refined manners, Ron and Betty Lovell had been cold, callous people who shouldn't have been allowed to parent any child. Ron had been an abusive drunk and Betty a woman who would do anything to maintain the perfect family façade, include ignore the verbal and psychological abuse she'd been subjected to from the minute she set foot in their home.

That had been her reality. Paint it any way and it still looked the same: miserable and depressing, a childhood filled with enough bad memories to last a lifetime. And by the vulnerability beneath the defiance she'd glimpsed on Molly's face, she would do anything to prevent the little girl she'd just met going through half of what she had.

"Listen, Brody. I'm an upstanding citizen. I pay my taxes. I run my own business, and anyone in this town can vouch for how much I love kids. Heard of *Fey For Fun*?"

He shook his head. "I haven't been here long and I've had my hands full settling the house and getting school organised for Molly."

At least she couldn't fault him for that. "I run the fairy shop. Kids love it."

She did too. It was her slice of magic in this all-round dreary world. Whether it be stocking the shelves with fairy dust or elves gold, the latest in pink tulle tutus or silver-spangled wings, she relished every part of her job. And when it came to dressing up for the local kids fairy parties, she absolutely, positively, had the best job in the world.

"Fairy shop?" His brows relaxed out of their frown to shoot skyward instead. He made it sound like she ran a brothel.

"The best this side of Sydney," she said, not knowing why she needed to justify the success of her business to this man. Besides, he looked like the type of guy who would scoff at anything make-believe.

"Fairies, huh?"

For a moment, she thought she glimpsed a softening around the corners of his mouth. However, the movement was gone in a flash so she must've imagined it.

She sighed and glanced at her watch. "Yes, fairies. And wizards and elves and Santas and Easter bunnies. You know, all the stuff a guy like you wouldn't believe in. Speaking of which, I need to find an Easter bunny urgently so if you'll excuse me?"

"A guy like me?"

"You don't strike me as the type to go in for magic stuff, that's all," she finished lamely, her attention captured by the spark of interest in his dark eyes.

"Is that right?"

She nodded, desperately trying to hide her surprise. If the glimpse of initial disapproval in his eyes had surprised her, it had nothing on the hint of a smile that played around his mouth. The guy could actually crack a smile?

"Well, in that case, I guess it's useless me trying to help you find this missing Easter bunny."

"He's not missing. He pulled out at the last minute and has left me in the lurch, not to mention thirty of the local kids."

She tried to ignore the sadness that swamped her, muttering "The rat," under her breath. Though her sadness had nothing to do with Prickly Pete exiting her life but more for the kids who'd been looking forward to the Easter pageant as much as she did and she hated to let them down.

"By the expression on your face, looks like that particular bunny is stewed the next time you see him."

And then it happened. Brody Elliott smiled and the effect was breathtaking, like the sun coming out from behind thunderous clouds, illuminating everything within its sphere and warming her in the same way, right down to her soul.

Trying to recover her wits, she said, "I won't be seeing him again. Not if he knows what's good for him."

His smile dimmed and he glanced away, oddly uncomfortable. Jeez, this guy really needed to loosen up. If smiling made him feel bad, he needed to practise more often.

"Sounds like you're in a bind."

His gaze returned to hers and he frowned, the angry indentation between his brows slipping into place with ease. Not that it marred his good looks. Nothing short of disastrous plastic surgery could do that but he appeared so much friendlier when he wasn't glowering at the world.

"Yeah, though it's the kids I feel sorry for."

Boy, could she relate. The nuns at the orphanage had talked up Santa's impending visit for an entire month before Christmas and though she'd been barely old enough to grasp the whole concept, she'd looked forward to his arrival with the fervent passion of a child who has nothing else to look forward to.

The man in the red suit with his treasure trove of presents had never arrived and she still remembered the acute emptiness that had made her sob her little heart out. Until she'd received a clip across the ears for her troubles.

"How big is the bunny suit?" He asked, offhand, as if it didn't mean much, though by the softening of his frown she'd hazard a guess he felt sorry for the kids as much as she did.

She looked him up and down, letting her gaze linger on all the right places—broad chest, firm abs, lean hips, long legs—before returning to meet his eyes with a cheeky grin.

"Big enough if you're volunteering."

"If the suit fits, guess I can lend a hand." His lips twitched and the spark that lit his eyes warmed her as much as his fleeting smile a few minutes earlier. He shrugged, as if stepping in at the last minute to save her was no big deal.

"For the kids," he added as an afterthought, as if he didn't want her getting the wrong idea that he was doing it for her.

Taking in his brooding frown, the surly curl of his lip and the casual slouch against the fence post, he sure didn't look like a knight in shining armour. Instead, he looked like a guy with the weight of the world on his broad shoulders and though it had nothing to do with her, she found herself wondering who or what had dumped it there.

"Thanks. The kids will really appreciate it."

And I do too, she thought, knowing her gratitude would

make him uncomfortable and instinctively keeping it to herself.

He straightened and thrust his hands in his pockets, the simple action outlining hard-packed pecs beneath the black cotton. Wow, the guy had some body, his superb upper torso more than a match for that sensational butt. Pity about the personality.

"I just have one more question."

Wrenching her mind from memories of the way his butt had looked bending over the car trunk earlier that week, she managed a squeaky, "Yeah?"

"When do I get to see you in a fairy costume?"

Before she could respond, he winked and strolled away, leaving her with a gloriously unimpeded view of the piece of anatomy she'd just been fantasising about.

Two

Brody sat in his car parked outside *Fey For Fun* and drummed his fingers against the steering wheel, wondering what on earth had prompted him to do this. He had enough problems of his own without stepping in to help out a bunch of kids he'd never met.

He should be at home right now, figuring out how to raise his own kid rather than secretly enjoying the brief taste of freedom from responsibility this afternoon would bring.

He closed his eyes, leaning back against the headrest. Molly was a bundle of energy, a constant source of amazement, consternation and worry in his otherwise drab life and he loved her to bits. He knew he fell short as a parent, his constant guilt at causing the death of her mother a burden that manifested itself in many ways, most of it directed at his beautiful daughter.

He'd turned into a taciturn grump and as much as he'd like to change his ways, he couldn't. Guilt did that to a man, a terrible all-consuming guilt that ripped at his soul on a daily basis, draining him until he had nothing left to give no matter how much he wanted to.

Poor Molly. He sure as hell wouldn't win any father of the year contests.

Now, to complicate matters, that interfering woman next door had coerced him into playing the Easter bunny. How stupid could he be?

Opening his eyes and looking through the glass shopfront, he had a fair idea. Real stupid, if his gut reaction was any indication as he caught a glimpse of his neighbour behind the counter, smiling and chatting with an old woman while she gift-wrapped a miniature set of fairies.

Carissa Lewis had a smile that could light up a room, and combined with the soft blonde curls framing her heart-shaped face, guileless blue eyes and a cheeky dimple that could tempt a saint, had him focussing on a woman in a way he hadn't in a long time.

He'd initially been annoyed she'd befriended Molly. His daughter had suffered enough loss in her brief life without growing attached to a woman who obviously could only offer an afternoon's entertainment. However, when he'd confronted Carissa, he'd been totally unprepared for his own reaction to the woman who looked like a cross between a naughty pixie and a temptress.

Awareness had flooded his body for the first time in years, making him more terse than usual. Instead of scaring her off as his abrupt manner did to most people, she'd stood up to him with something akin to challenge in her fathomless blue eyes and he'd been prompted to do all sorts of uncharacteristic things, like play knight in shining armour and volunteer to spend an afternoon sweating in a bunny suit.

Of all the stupid things he'd ever done, that had to come close to the top. Apart from the stupidest decision of them all, the one where he'd pulled over a speeding driver all those years ago and let the kid go with a warning, only to stare into that cocky face two years later when the jerk had been charged with vehicular manslaughter for killing Jackie, his wife, in a head-on collision while speeding again.

Yeah, that topped the list of dumbest things he'd ever done and he'd been paying for it every day since.

A loud tapping on his window brought him back to the present.

"Are you going to sit out here snoozing all day?" Carissa mouthed the words through the glass and he stifled the urge to re-start the engine, floor the accelerator and head for home.

The woman looked good enough to eat, her simple outfit of white flowing trousers and pink fitted top accentuating her piquant beauty in its simplicity. On any other woman the combination would've looked plain. On her, it looked stunning.

He wracked his brain for an excuses to leave as the window slid down, only to be bowled over again as a subtle waft of rose essence blew into the car. He'd always liked roses and had brought a bunch home for Jackie on a regular basis, and though she'd always thanked him, he could tell she wasn't a big fan. Jackie preferred fancy orchids to simple roses but she'd been too polite to say otherwise.

Everything about his wife had been fancy, from her manicured fingernails to her elegant clothes and he still wondered what she'd ever seen in a middle-class cop from the wrong side of the tracks.

"Hey." Carissa snapped her fingers in front of his face. "You better pay closer attention when you're with the kids, otherwise they'll whip those chocolate eggs out of your basket in no time at all."

"Look, about the kids—"

"Come on, we haven't got long to get you dressed and into the garden out the back of the shop for the egg hunt." She opened the car door, grabbed hold of his hand and all but tugged him out.

He should've blurted out any old excuse. He should've slammed the door shut, started the engine and left her standing there. Instead, at the first touch of her hand on his, all thought of abandoning her fled and he found himself being led into her shop, wondering what it was about this woman that made him want to jump through hoops.

"Thanks for doing this. I really appreciate it," she said, pushing open the door to her shop and releasing his hand.

"Wow," was all he could manage as he took in the filmy pink gauze draped around the shop, the silver stars spangling on a midnight ceiling, and a staggering array of fairies, elves, goblins, wizards, frogs and princesses in every shape, texture and size.

If he was a kid he'd never want to leave this place. As a grown-up, he was intrigued by this enigmatic woman and hated himself for it. He didn't have the time or inclination to waste on another woman. Molly was the only female in his life these days and he intended to keep it that way.

"Feel free to look around." She waved him away with a small hand devoid of jewellery and he found himself startled by another comparison to Jackie, who had worn rings with priceless gems dripping from every finger.

"Where's the suit?" He muttered, and by her narrow-eyed glare he knew he sounded testy. "I thought we needed to get this show on the road?"

Though he softened his tone she hadn't lost the wary look that had crept into her eyes when he'd practically barked at her and he resisted the urge to apologise. Besides, what did he have to apologise for? He spoke like this all the time and if his nosy neighbour didn't like it, too bad. He wouldn't be seeing her much after today so what was the big deal?

Shame on you, Brody Elliott. Mind your manners.

He blinked in surprise at the echo of his wife's phrase. During their brief marriage, he'd often felt like a gauche boy being chastised by the lady of the house and any love he'd had for his society wife had soon waned while his love for Molly, the reason they'd married in the first place, grew daily.

Everyone had been right. Jackie had made him pay for getting her pregnant even though he'd used protection, and though he'd done the right thing by her their marriage had been based on guilt from the start. His guilt.

Guilt at ruining Jackie's life, according to her snobby family.

Guilt at robbing her of a life on easy street if she'd married the right man from her socio-economic sphere.

Guilt at how much he blamed her for losing his freedom.

And for the last four years, the gut-wrenching guilt he'd killed her.

"If you don't want to do this, I'll understand," Carissa said, the concern in her eyes reaching out and enveloping him in a warm embrace, no matter how unwelcome.

Damn it. As a cop, he'd been a master at the poker face. It had been one of the skills that had kept him at the top of his game. However, like everything else in his life, he'd let his job slide and looked like his skills had followed suit.

Slipping his poor-excuse-for-a-poker-face into place, he said, "I'm ready. Where's the suit?"

"Out the back. Follow me."

As he walked behind her, struggling to keep his eyes averted from the way her butt moved beneath the soft white cotton of her pants and failing miserably, he wondered for the hundredth time in the last hour if he'd lost his mind.

———

Chapter 3

Carissa was proud of her ability to read people. She'd mastered the skill from an early age, learning to blend into the background in the hope to avoid drawing attention to herself and earning a harsh word or cruel putdown from her stepdad Ron in the process. Being able to blend allowed her the freedom to observe people, to look, listen and pick up on non-verbal cues.

Yet as she watched Brody cavorting with the children like he was born to the role of Easter bunny, she had no idea what to make of her new neighbour.

"Looks like your bunny is doing a good job with the kids," Tahnee, her younger sister said, plopping into a garden chair next to her. "Didn't know Pete had it in him."

"It's not Peter." Carissa wrinkled her nose as if she'd just smelt something nasty. In this case, *eau d'dumped*.

Tahnee's astute gaze fixed on her in an instant. "Trouble in paradise?"

"Being with Peter was never paradise," Carissa muttered, knowing she'd hung around their dead-end relationship for eight months for one reason and one reason only. Familiarity. And in her case, it definitely bred contempt.

"Yay." Tahnee clapped her hands and bounced in her seat. "Bye-bye to the loser. I knew he wasn't worthy of you."

"Why didn't you say something earlier?"

Tahnee rolled her eyes, the exact shade of blue as hers, and once again Carissa was struck by the likeness between the three Lewis girls, thankful they'd found each other after all these years. In fact, she never would've set up shop here in Stockton if it hadn't been for Tahnee. When they'd been reunited, she'd been so thrilled to finally have a loving family again that she'd moved to the small town two hours north of Sydney just to be closer to her sister, who had lived here for years.

Tahnee snickered. "Because I don't interfere in my sister's relationships, as much as I'd like to."

"Speaking of which, have you heard from Kristen? Mick spirited her away for a week in Perth before she heads back to Singapore and I haven't heard from her."

"Another loser," Tahnee snorted. "Miserly Mick, that is. Bet Kristen's the one springing for the holiday, not the other way around. That guy has long pockets and short arms when it comes to spending money."

Carissa chuckled and happened to agree with her sister. "As long as she's happy."

"Mark my words. Kristen will be joining us in happy singledom in a few weeks if I'm not mistaken. Spending more than a few hours with that creep will open her eyes quick-smart."

"We'll see," Carissa murmured, her attention suddenly diverted by the amazing sight of the Easter bunny grappling with Timmy Fields, a gorgeous little blond boy who'd lost both parents recently and had her empathising.

"Hey, Timmy. Take it easy on the Easter bunny. You might pull his ears off."

Though maybe that wouldn't be such a bad idea? Might get brooding Brody to listen to her for all of two seconds. He'd barely spoken more than a few words to her since they'd met and she still hadn't convinced him to let Molly spend some time with her.

That little girl needed some attention and she was just the woman to give it to her. It didn't take an Einstein to figure out Molly needed some TLC: from her dishevelled appearance to her defiant attitude, Molly craved affection and if her father spoke to her like he did to everyone else...poor Molly.

"So who's in the bunny costume?" Tahnee unwrapped a chocolate Easter egg and popped it in her mouth. "Mmm... heaven. Actually, I should've known it wasn't Pete. This bunny is way too tall and broad-shouldered to be Puny Pete."

"Meet bunny Brody Elliott, my new neighbor."

Tahnee sat up so quickly she almost tipped out of her chair. "*The* Brody Elliott?"

"Uh-huh. Heard of him?"

"Heard of him?" Tahnee's voice rose and Carissa shushed her. "Sis, where have you been hiding? Don't you listen to the Stockton grapevine?"

"Don't have time."

"Your loss."

Maybe she could make an exception in this case? "So tell me about *the* Brody Elliott."

"He's an ex-cop, lived in Sydney his whole life. Has a real bad boy reputation." Tahnee leaned closer and lowered her voice to an almost-whisper, no mean feat for her loud, brash sibling. "Knocked up some society chick, married her, had a child who he adores. Then, the wife dies about four years ago when the girl is a toddler and he's raised her on his own since. Carries a huge chip on his shoulder, like he blames the world for his problems."

Carissa shook her head and stared wide-eyed at her sister, knowing if the rumour mills were true what she'd just heard about Brody went a long way to explaining his grumpy manner. Sounded like he'd had a rough time and then some. "Where did you hear all that?"

"Daisy Smythe is the dead wife's aunt. That's one of the reasons he's come to live here, so that his daughter can get some female influence in her life. Old Daisy told Pat at the pharmacy and I overheard the whole thing."

"You mean you eavesdropped?"

Tahnee had the grace to blush. "It wasn't like the old duck was talking in whispers or anything."

"You're unbelievable."

"So, how did you get big bad Brody to be your bunny? Tell all."

Carissa remembered the look on Molly's cute face when they'd first met and Brody's subsequent glower. She could hardly believe the taciturn man had found it in his heart to volunteer to help her out, let alone throw himself wholeheartedly into the task if his current wrestling match with half a dozen of the cherubs was any indication.

She shrugged, not wanting to add fuel to Tahnee's thirst for news. "Looks like the guy has a soft spot for kids so once he heard I needed help, he put his hand up."

"Really?"

Carissa understood her sister's scepticism. If what Tahnee had learned from Daisy was true, and what she'd observed first hand in his general demeanour, the guy didn't exactly strike a welcoming cord with everyone he met.

Not that she put much stock in anything old Daisy said. Daisy Smythe, a straight-laced spinster who'd lived in Stockton her entire life and shunned anyone she considered 'foreign'— even those who came from Sydney, a scant two hours away— was notorious for her shallow views. And this was the woman Brody had chosen to be the female influence in his daughter's life?

"He seems nice enough," Carissa said, trying to forget

exactly how *nice* Brody was, particularly some of his impressive physical attributes.

"Wish I could see him without that costume." Tahnee popped another egg into her mouth and delicately licked chocolate from her fingertips like a kitten lapping up the last of its cream. "I like bad boys."

"He has a daughter to raise. I doubt Brody would be up for a fling, especially in a small town like this."

"Ooh." Tahnee's eyes narrowed as she fixed her perceptive gaze on Carissa. "You sound mighty sure of what the man wants. Something you're not telling me, Sis? Like you've got dibs on him? Little wonder Puny Pete is out of the picture."

"For your information, Peter dumped me, not the other way around. And I haven't got dibs on anyone." Her interest in Brody Elliott stemmed from a desire to make his daughter's life easier, not some ill-placed lust for him. "He's my neighbour. I'm just helping him get acquainted with the town."

Tahnee's grin spoke volumes. "*Riiight.* Thousands wouldn't believe you, Sis, but I will." She stood in one, lithe movement and Carissa lamented that her two gorgeous sisters had got all the height genes in the Lewis family. She barely made it past five foot in heels.

"Anyway, I better dash. I have a deadline to meet and my editor waits for no-one. Later." Tahnee kissed her cheek and strolled from the garden, a tall, slim blonde in hipster jeans and matching denim jacket.

Yeah, her sister was beautiful all right and if she ever set her sights on Brody, he'd be toast.

And she'd be greener than Fred and all his froggy cohorts put together.

Glancing at her watch, she realised the last hour had flown. Brody had done such a good job entertaining the kids she'd hardly had to do anything, including call on her back-up plan of distributing mass amounts of choccie eggs if the bunny had been too moody to play.

Thankfully, the bunny had been one hop ahead of her all afternoon and it had been a pleasure seeing him bring joy to so many little faces. She loved this motley bunch of kids ranging in age from four to nine, all locals whose parents visited her shop on a regular basis looking for gifts.

She'd been hired to organise fairy parties for all the little girls in town over the last few years and knew almost every kid in Stockton personally, which is why she went the extra yard at Easter and Christmas, organising the Pageant and Santa's cave for the darlings.

Clapping her hands, she called the children to her. "Okay, time for the Easter bunny to go. What do we say to the bunny?"

"Thank you, Easter bunny. Come again next year," thirty voices rang out in unison in the peculiar monotone they'd rehearsed a few hours ago.

Brody waved to the kids and hopped toward the back door of the shop. She smiled at him, wondering if he could see her through the peepholes in the rabbit's mouth. In response, he turned, wiggled his cute little cotton tail butt at her and hopped into the shop, shutting the door behind him.

Well, well, well. Maybe there was more to brooding Brody than he let on?

Chapter 4

"You didn't have to do this."

Brody glanced at the table Carissa had set for dinner and wanted to bolt home. It looked too cosy, too inviting and far too scary for his peace of mind.

He didn't do dinners. He didn't do dates.

And this meal she'd cooked as thanks for him helping her out with the bunny thing looked like a frightening combination of both.

She turned from the stove, brandishing a wooden spoon filled with rich bolognaise sauce in one hand and a fairy-covered pot holder in the other. "I know, but I wanted to. It's the least I could do after the show you put on for the kids yesterday."

He managed to look affronted for all of two seconds. "That wasn't a show."

Far from it. He'd enjoyed himself more than he had in ages acting like a goofball with the kids, enjoying their rough-house tactics. He never played like that with Molly, too scared he'd hurt her. She was all he had left in this world and he'd do his best to protect her—after doing such a lousy job with her mum.

"Really?" She tasted the sauce and smiled, a self-satisfied smirk of a cook who knows she's good and is proud of it.

Despite his wariness of this whole situation, his mouth watered at the spicy aromas wafting through the small kitchen: a rich combination of garlic, tomatoes, oregano and basil infused the air, and he wondered if he'd ever smelt anything so tempting.

Or seen anything so tempting, as he watched Carissa turn back to the stove, the simple movement causing the short black skirt she wore to flip around her knees in a provocative swish. She was barefoot, her shapely calves beckoning him to feel their contours and keep heading north to the hidden delights underneath that flirty skirt.

He swore silently and thrust his hands in his pockets, feeling more uncomfortable by the minute.

What the hell was he doing here?

He needed to escape. Fast.

"The bunny act was nothing and this really isn't necessary. So thanks anyway, but I need to check on Molly." He sidled toward the door, unprepared for the flash of anger in her eyes as she swung around to face him.

"I thought you said Molly is with Daisy."

"Yeah, she is."

"And didn't you also say she adores her great aunt?"

He nodded, feeling like a fool. What harm could a simple meal do? He could eat and run. Besides, Molly had raved about the great time she'd had at Daisy's yesterday afternoon and had been more than eager to spend a few hours with her this evening. Thankfully, old Daisy had become an ally of his since he'd moved to town and it didn't take a genius to figure out the old lady's softened stance had to do with him wanting Molly to bond with her great aunt.

The way he looked at it, the severe spinster would be a good influence on Molly, giving her some female stability in her topsy-turvy world. The world he'd upended through his stupidity at letting that brash young driver off the hook. He'd seen something of himself in that guy—confident, cocky, with the gift of the gab—and he'd taken the soft option.

Pity the soft option had turned out to be the hardest one for his motherless daughter.

As for dinner, he could do this. As long as his long-dormant libido didn't get any crazy ideas. In four years, he hadn't looked sideways at a woman and now he finally felt settled for the first time in ages, maybe his imagination had been hot-wired into action? Though it probably had more to do with the surprising woman wearing a fitted I Luv Chocolate T-shirt, a short skirt and no shoes than anything else.

"It's settled then. You uncork the wine, I'll serve." She thrust a corkscrew into his hands before he could change his mind and all but pushed him into a seat at the table. "Hope you like shiraz. I've been saving this."

"Don't open it on my account."

"I love a good red so go ahead."

Carissa almost bit her tongue in frustration. She was trying to be nice here, to repay Brody for helping her out with the kids, but it wasn't working. Dinner with her moody neighbor had been a bad idea. He obviously didn't want to be here and she hated having to watch her p's and q's.

Hoping an innocuous comment would break the awkward silence that enveloped them, she said, "Tell me about your job."

"I'm not working at the moment." He poured the wine into glasses and handed one to her, his frown a clear indication he didn't want to discuss his employment status further.

Undeterred, she smiled, determined to get him to lighten up, to give her a glimpse of the man behind the terse façade.

She knew he'd had a hard time and there was something about Brody Elliott that had her wanting to hug him, pat his back and make it all better. "I heard you were a cop before you came to Stockton?"

"Who told you that?"

"You know what small towns are like. Everyone knows everyone else's business."

Laying his wine down on the table after taking a healthy swig, he folded his arms and leaned against the bench top. "Yeah, but I wish they'd butt out of mine. Being a cop is in the past and I'd like to keep it that way. What else are they saying about me?"

Dishing up the pasta and sauce, she wished she hadn't gone down this track. Perhaps she was rushing things, pushing him for private information too soon? He'd probably clam up for good and then she'd never get anything out of him.

"That you're a widower."

"That's true. Jackie died four years ago."

Not surprised he didn't volunteer more information, she bustled about the kitchen before she pried any further—like asking how it happened—laying the meal on the table and ushering him to sit before she joined him.

"It must've been awfully hard for you and Molly."

He nodded and offered her the salad while he broke off a chunk of garlic bread. "Molly was barely two. One of the few words she spoke at that time was mum and she walked around for month's afterwards saying 'mum gone'. It was heartbreaking." He stuffed the bread in his mouth and she wasn't sure if she heard correctly when he muttered, "Still is."

"I'm sorry," she said, for the loss he'd suffered and for the pain that obviously still hung over him like a dark cloud.

He must've loved his wife very much and if anyone could understand the long-term affects of grief, she could. There wasn't a day that went by that she didn't think about her parents and what her life would've been like if they'd lived. "I know how Molly feels. I lost both my parents when I was three. I was devastated."

A flare of interest sparked his eyes as he fixed that all-seeing gaze on her. "What happened?"

"Dad was a geologist and loved travelling the world. Mum accompanied him on a trip to the Alps, probably for a break from the three of us. They died in an avalanche."

"I'm sorry too," he murmured, his genuine sympathy bringing an unexpected lump to her throat.

She'd had years to come to terms with her grief, long years when she cried herself to sleep every night while huddled beneath the blankets trying to stifle her sobs from her angry adoptive father, yet here she was, about to blubber in front of a virtual stranger who'd offered a kind word.

Sensing her distress, he cleared his throat. "You said three of us?"

"I have two sisters. Tahnee's the youngest and Kristen's the oldest. They split us up at the orphanage. Tahnee and Kristen got adopted out first, I spent a year in that hellhole. We found each other about six years ago."

"Crap," he said, taking hold of her hand across the table. "How awful."

Grasping her hand had to be a purely instinctive gesture but the minute his hand enveloped hers, she couldn't think straight. His touch elicited a response she couldn't comprehend. It was far too early to feel anything other than respect for this man, respect for a single father doing the best he could in raising his daughter.

She slid her hand out from his on the pretext of dishing up and managed a weak smile. "Listen to us, a real pair of agony aunts." She handed him a plate, careful to avoid touching him again. Otherwise, he'd probably end up wearing hot pasta on his crotch. "Here, try this. It's my favorite recipe."

Casting a quizzical glance her way, he took the plate she offered. "Thanks. Smells delicious."

They dug into their meal, only pausing to make the odd casual remark like "pass the Parmesan please" or "more dressing on your salad?" She would've liked more conversation but as meals went, it wasn't the worst she'd had with a man. In fact, there was something strangely comforting about a guy who didn't feel obliged to babble about his business or sporting prowess all through dinner, who seemed happy to eat in companionable silence without spouting off.

"Thanks for the meal. I'll help you clean up then it's time I left." He stood so quickly his chair teetered on two wooden legs before slamming back on the floor.

"What's your hurry? We haven't had dessert yet."

He patted his stomach, drawing her attention to the hard planes evident beneath the white cotton T-shirt and putting a new slant on *dessert* in her mind. "I'll pass. Thanks for a magnificent meal. Now, do you want to wash or dry?"

"Leave it. I'll use the dishwasher," she said, turning away before he saw the wistful expression on her face.

She didn't want him to leave.

She wanted him to stay and share dessert, perhaps talk some more, maybe even laugh a little? They were neighbors and it wouldn't hurt to be on friendly terms. Who knew, he might even lighten up and let her spend some time with Molly? Though by the return of his surly expression, she doubted it.

"Here. I packed extra for you and Molly to have tomorrow." She held out a plastic container, surprised by the resentment that flashed across his face.

"Thanks, but we're fine. I can cook, you know."

"I never said you couldn't." The food grew heavy in her hand and her outstretched arm drooped. "I just thought Molly might like some of this."

"Molly is fine."

Anger shot through her body, surprising in its intensity. Carissa rarely lost her temper, viewing anger as a wasted emotion for the gutless—like her adoptive father who'd wielded it every chance he got.

Brody's defensiveness annoyed her. So the guy had a massive chip on his shoulder? No need for everyone around him to suffer.

"I didn't say she wasn't."

"Whatever. I better go."

Damn, he was touchy. She hadn't seem him around his daughter but if this is how he spoke to Molly, it went a long way to explaining the wary look in the little girl's eyes she'd glimpsed the other day when they'd first met.

"You do that." Their gazes locked, his angry, hers challenging. She'd stare him down if it killed her, the big grump.

"Thanks for dinner. I'll let myself out." He headed for the door, almost wrenching the knob off in his hurry to leave.

"Brody, any time Molly wants to play over here is fine by me. Just send her over."

If she could do anything to bring a spark to the little girl's world, she would. From what she could see, Molly spent far too much time alone in her backyard, perched in that giant eucalyptus, with a glum expression on her cheeky face. At first appearance, Molly seemed a lonely girl who needed attention and if anyone knew how that felt, she did. Ron and Betty had ignored her from the minute she'd set foot in their impressive house and though she'd wanted for nothing materially, emotionally she'd craved affection.

She'd been the model daughter, yearning for a kind word or gentle caress from her new parents. And what had she got for her trouble? Harsh putdowns and scathing verbal attacks that gave her nightmares to this day.

Molly must've been too young to remember much of her

mother but loneliness was an emotion that could strike at any age and if she could do anything to alleviate the little girl's pain, she would. If the occasional play session could brighten Molly's day, she'd stand up to big bad Brody every day of the week to get her way.

"Why the interest in my daughter?" His fierce gaze didn't scare her. Not much, that is.

"I love kids and Molly's new in town." She shrugged, as if his response didn't mean much when she hoped he had the sense to take her honest answer at face value and give her a chance to get to know Molly. "Guess I thought she could use some friends."

His frown lessened for about two seconds before he muttered, "We'll see," and walked out the door.

"We'll see," she imitated under her breath, shaking her head and trying not to break plates as she shoved them into the dishwasher.

Three

"Daddy, is it okay if I make hot cross buns with Carissa? She has to make a whole heap for Easter and she needs my help. She has flour and sugar and a special big mixing bowl and everything. Can I? Please, Daddy? Please?"

Brody rubbed the spot between his eyes, the one that permanently ached these days, and looked down at his daughter hopping from one foot to the other. Her blue eyes sparkled but a dirty smudge streaked down the side of her face, one plait had come undone, her dress was buttoned up wrong and a buckle on her Mary-Jane's had come loose.

Hell, she looked like a neglected kid. Molly deserved so much more than he could give but right now he could barely face each day let alone pay constant attention to his daughter. He was tired, so damn tired. Tired of the long, endless days, tired of having no focus, and worst of all, tired of the never-ending guilt that he'd deprived his precious girl of her mother.

Despite the passing years, it didn't get any easier. Nothing sparked his interest any more and if it weren't for Molly he probably would've become a beach bum by now, living like a hermit in the far north tropics, not seeing another soul for years on end.

But he couldn't run away. He had responsibilities, the main one currently staring up at him with those brilliant blue eyes so like her mother's.

"Okay, but don't be too long. You need to have a bath before dinner."

"But Carissa said we could eat the buns for dinner?" Molly pouted, another action reminiscent of Jackie, who'd made an art-form out of it in an attempt to get her own way.

He sighed, deciding to give in this once. He'd gone out of his way to avoid his nosy neighbour since she cooked him that thank-you dinner, not in the mood to make polite small talk with someone he had no intention of seeing any more than necessary. However, Carissa seemed like a woman with a steady head on her shoulders and from what he'd seen at the Easter pageant she was good with kids. Perhaps it wouldn't hurt to let Molly befriend her? After all, why let Molly suffer because of his anti-social personality?

"Sure thing, munchkin. You can eat the buns for dinner."

"Yay Daddy, you're the best!" Molly flung herself at him and he scooped her up, snuggling into her as she wrapped her arms around his neck, his heart filled with love, his head wishing he could be a better father, the type of father she deserved.

"But not too many, okay? Otherwise, you might get a tummy ache."

Molly's eyes widened and her nose wrinkled, obviously remembering her last attack of the gripes. She'd moaned for what seemed like hours and he'd felt totally and utterly helpless, waiting for the paracetamol to kick in.

So what was new? He usually felt helpless around her anyway.

"I promise to only eat two." She held up her fingers and

counted. "One. Two. See? Only this many won't give me a tummy ache, will it?"

Chuckling, he dropped a kiss on her nose. "Two will be just fine. I'll come and get you from Carissa's in an hour, so be good."

She slid off his lap and sent him a reproachful stare. "I'm always good. Bye." With a quick wave, she ran out the door and skipped across the front lawn to Carissa's, where the woman bent down and enveloped her in a hug before beckoning her inside.

Brody braced against the windowsill, pleased he hadn't lost his astute eye for character assessment. It had been a bonus as a cop, not that he had much use for those skills these days. Carissa had known Molly less than a week and she'd welcomed his little girl into her life with no expectations, no demands, and the sight of her embracing Molly left him thankful he'd made a correct decision for once.

Interestingly, Carissa had shown more interest in Molly in seven days than Jackie had in the first eighteen months of Molly's life. Jackie had been a lousy mum and though she'd loved their little girl in her own way, she hadn't a maternal bone in her model-thin body. Probably another reason which slowly but surely killed what little affection he'd had for her when they'd first married.

Grateful for an hour's respite from his whirlwind daughter, he headed for the shower. However, he didn't get very far as an ear-piercing scream ripped through the dusk and it came straight from Carissa's.

Silently praying that nothing had happened to Molly, he vaulted the picket fence between their homes and ran through Carissa's front door. Another high-pitched scream from the kitchen had him tearing through her doll-like house at breakneck speed, his heart in his mouth.

He'd stopped believing in a higher power around the time

he lost Jackie but now found himself making bargains with the great man.

Please let Molly be safe. I couldn't handle losing her too. She's everything to me. I'll be a better person, I promise, starting with being a better father. And being nicer to my neighbour.

In the split second it took him to recite his plea bargain he burst into the kitchen, scanning the scene with years of practice as a police officer: check for danger, eliminate risk, make the environment safe.

During his years on the force, he'd faced armed robbers, drug addicts stoned out of their brains and even the odd murderer. He thought he'd seen it all and would be prepared for any contingency. However, staring at the scene in front of him, he knew he'd been wrong.

"Come on, Carissa, hop down. It'll be okay. He won't hurt you." Molly stood next to the bench top, tugging insistently on Carissa's hand while his neighbour cowered on the bench, both feet tucked under her skirt with her face covered in flour.

Carissa shook her head furiously, sending a cloud of flour into the air around her, floating like a nimbus. "Uh-uh. He could still be under the table."

Molly giggled and tugged on Carissa's hand harder. "No, silly. I saw him run behind that cupboard and into that little hole. Wanna take a look?"

"No!" Carissa wriggled back on the bench top and scrunched her legs up further if that were possible.

The tension drained from Brody's body and trying not to laugh he stepped into Carissa's line of vision. "Everything okay in here?"

Carissa fixed him with a withering stare. "Does it look okay to you?"

"Daddy, I saw a mouse! He ran straight across the floor and under that cupboard. He was real quick but Carissa got scared and hopped up there and now she won't come down." Molly had released Carissa's hand and raced across the kitchen to grab his. "Come and help her down. I don't think she listens to kids."

Stifling a grin, he allowed his daughter to lead him to Carissa. "Afraid of mice, huh?"

"Smart deduction, wise guy." She slid toward the edge of the bench and he reached out, placed both hands on her hips, and lifted her to the floor.

She weighed next to nothing and his hands moulded to her waist snugly. He'd never had a thing for petite woman but try telling that to his dormant hormones.

"Thanks." Her hands rested on his chest, the heat from her palms scorching through the cotton of his polo shirt.

He needed to release her. Instead, he stood there like one of the stuffed mannequins the cops used to practice their tackles on, staring down at her. Even with her face covered in flour, her curls tumbling in riotous waves and an apron string draped around an ear, she looked beautiful.

And the urge to kiss her shocked the hell out of him.

"Isn't my dad the best, Carissa?" Molly plopped onto a chair, legs swinging, and picked up a wooden spoon to resume bun-making duties.

"He sure is," Carissa murmured, her wide-eyed blue gaze never leaving his for a second, making him feel like a superhero.

Clearing his throat, he managed a weak smile as he stepped away, breaking the weird spell that held them enthralled while they touched. "I didn't do much. Looks like Molly had the situation under control."

Molly nodded and brandished her spoon like a sword. "I love mice. I tried to tell Carissa that but she kept making really loud screeching noises, like the ones you don't like me making, Daddy."

To his amusement, Carissa blushed beneath her flour coating, the faint pink staining her cheeks adding to the pretty picture she made, even dusted in the white stuff.

"It's a stupid phobia I've had forever." Her voice dropped to a whisper to protect Molly from hearing how her new friend detested mice. "Sorry about the screaming."

Before he could question his action, he reached out and brushed her cheek. "Hey, don't worry about it. I'm used to rescuing damsels in distress, remember? Even if this cop hung up his badge ages ago."

Her blush deepened and for one, crazy second he thought she'd lean into his hand. Hell, he wanted her to. He wanted to caress her cheek, to feel the heat beneath the surface of her porcelain skin.

Had he lost his mind?

There was no room in his life for anyone other than Molly and even she was proving a handful. Yet for one tiny, infinite moment he wanted this woman and the knowledge slammed into his consciousness like a blast from a detonated bomb. He hoped the results wouldn't be as devastating.

Dropping his hand as if burned, he said, "Guess the bun-making exercise is off?"

"No way. Molly and I are committed, aren't we, sweetie?"

At her name, Molly looked up from the recipe book she'd been flipping through and Brody smiled, recognising the determined glint in his daughter's eyes. Molly had a mind of her own and once made up, he had a damn difficult time swaying her.

"Yep. I wanna make hot cross buns. And you said I could eat two for dinner, Daddy. You promised."

Carissa grinned in triumph and Brody knew when he was beaten. "Well, I'll leave you to it, then. Just holler if you see a you-know-what scamper across the floor again."

"Why don't you and Molly stay for dinner? I'll ring for a

pizza, that way I can shower and we'll make the buns afterwards\." She grimaced as she swiped at her face, coming away with a dusting of flour on her hands. "I must look a fright."

You look beautiful is what he thought.

"Won't take you long to get cleaned up," is what he said.

It had been way too long since he'd had female company and it showed. For a guy who used to have a way with words, he sure made a hash of things whenever he exchanged more than a hi with Carissa. Not that he had any intention of exchanging more than a few words with her. Getting involved wasn't on his agenda and never would be.

His reaction to her earlier had been purely chemical, a celibate guy attracted to a beautiful woman, nothing more, nothing less. Chemicals he could handle, it was the emotional stuff he could without. Either way, it was time to retreat.

"Thanks for the invitation but I'll leave you ladies to it. Molly, behave. I'll be back in an hour."

He sent a curt nod Carissa's way, waved at his daughter and all but ran out the door.

Damn, why couldn't he live next to a crotchety old bachelor like himself rather than a vibrant young woman? Logically, he knew nothing could ever happen between them, he wouldn't let it. Physically, his body could do without the temptation. Emotionally, he was too drained to give anyone apart from Molly anything.

And he would sure as hell keep it that way.

Four

Carissa ordered a pizza, had a quick shower while Molly watched a movie, and tried not to dither over how she looked.

She never dithered, especially over her appearance. She dressed for comfort not style and as for make-up, she rarely used the stuff. Yet here she was, her lashes mascaraed, her lips glossed and wearing her favourite clingy blue singlet top, the one that accentuated what little assets she had.

Not only that, she'd dabbed her favourite rose perfume behind her ears. And for what? On the off chance Brody would actually look at her for more than two seconds when he came to pick up Molly later?

The guy was totally immune to her and she should be glad. After her string of loser boyfriends she had no intention of going near a man for a long time. It didn't take a genius to figure out why she always had to have a guy in her life: a case of "a little affection is better than none" syndrome, hanging onto whatever she could get after having zero love growing up.

But not anymore. The next time she fell for a guy, she'd

make sure he gave her a lifetime of love. She deserved it and she'd be damned if she settled for anything less.

So what was she doing preening for a guy who didn't acknowledge her existence other than as his daughter's playmate? Simple. She may have wised up when it came to the male species but that didn't mean she wasn't a tad vain and after he'd seen her earlier, looking like a snowman and a quivering one to boot, she needed to make a better impression.

"Carissa, the pizza's here," Molly yelled from the kitchen and Carissa poked her tongue out at her reflection, trying to erase the memory of that loaded moment with Brody in the kitchen earlier, knowing the spark she'd glimpsed in his eyes had been a figment of her imagination but unable to forget it.

So what if she wanted to test his reaction by wearing something other than her usual drab stuff? Nothing wrong with seeing if the man had a pulse.

"Carissa! Come on!"

As she opened her bedroom door, a whirlwind of flying pigtails and flaying arms grabbed her legs and hung on. "I'm starving. Are you ready?"

"Sure am. I'm starving too. Let's eat." Bending down to hug Molly, she blinked back the sudden sting of tears as she enveloped the warm little body in her arms.

This is what she wanted out of life. Unconditional love.

Her friends wanted high-powered careers, slick men and loads of money. Give her the no-strings-attached love of a child any day.

And the genuine love of a good man, but she banished that thought as soon as it popped into her head.

No use wishing for a miracle. Especially as she'd given up on those a long time ago, around the time her adoptive father locked her in the closet to 'teach her a lesson'. She'd been Molly's age at the time and could add claustrophobia to her mouse-phobia courtesy of the mean old coot.

Shrugging out of the embrace, Molly skipped ahead of her to the kitchen. "Pizza and buns. My favourites."

After paying the delivery guy, who glared at her for making him wait, Carissa hoisted Molly onto a chair before sliding into one next to her and laying a generous slice on the little girl's plate. "Here you go, sweetie. Eat up."

"Yummy." Molly clapped her hands in glee, took a big bite out of her slice and grinned, an olive stuck in the gap where her front tooth used to be.

Carissa laughed, enjoying the simple pleasure of watching Molly devour the pizza slice like she hadn't eaten in a month.

"That was so yum," Molly said, licking mozzarella from her fingers. "Daddy doesn't let me have pizza very often. He makes me eat yucky things like broccoli and sprouts. Gross."

Carissa happened to agree with Molly about the veggie thing but decided to keep that particular bit of knowledge to herself. "Your dad wants you to grow big and strong, that's why it's important to eat stuff like that."

Molly wrinkled her nose and studied her with wide eyes. "That's what he says. How come you know so much about kids? Are you a mum?"

Carissa's heart clenched at the serious expression on Molly's face and she chose her words carefully in response. "I love kids, Molly. I get to play with them all the time through my job at the fairy shop. And though I'm not a mum right now, I'd like to be one day."

She'd love to have at least three of the little cherubs and she'd do a damn sight better job of parenting than Betty Lovell did with her. How that woman had turned a blind eye to her husband's drunken mean streak still left Carissa wanting to throttle her. A mother nurtured, protected and cherished her child. Betty had provided for her basic needs but as for protecting her from Ron's foul mouth or cherishing her with the love she'd so desperately craved, she'd been useless.

People needed a licence to drive a car, a licence to operate machinery, even a licence to fish, and she often wished people like the Lovells needed to undergo some sort of test to obtain a licence before parenting.

"I don't have a mummy." Molly's soft words wrenched her back to the present and she reached for the little girl instinctively, wanting to reassure her that everything would be all right despite only having one parent—and a grouchy one at that.

"Your mummy's in heaven, sweetheart and that means she's always with you, watching over you, no matter where you are." Carissa cuddled Molly close and she seemed quite content to snuggle into her arms, which only reinforced Carissa's suspicions regarding Brody.

If the guy treated everyone him like a potential enemy, how did he show love to his daughter? Did he cuddle her, comfort her, give her the affection she obviously craved? For Molly's sake, she hoped so.

"I know she's in heaven," Molly said, resting her head on Carissa's shoulder. "Daddy told me. I can't remember much about mummy but daddy does. He's really sad she's not with us anymore. I try to give him hugs to make him feel better but he's still sad a lot. I can tell because he makes a face like this."

Molly wriggled out of Carissa's arms, sat back on her chair, frowned and compressed her lips in an accurate imitation of her father's usual grim expression and Carissa struggled not to laugh.

Though there was nothing remotely funny that this darling child could sense Brody's discontent with the world. How long would it take before Molly started associating Brody's moodiness with her and reacting accordingly? The little girl was bright, sweet and affectionate and didn't need to shoulder her father's problems, nor take responsibility for something beyond her control.

So Brody still loved his wife and carried his grief around like a boulder around his neck? No reason to push away everyone around him, particularly his daughter. Why couldn't he see what was right in front of him? And though it was none of her business, she was sorely tempted to march next door right this minute and tell him how his surliness was affecting his daughter.

"Sometimes grown ups are sad, Molly and sometimes they're happy. And when they're happy, they do this." Carissa's fingers crawled across her lap and marched towards Molly's ribs, launching into a tickling session that left the little girl giggling and squirming and tickling her right back.

Thankfully, the diversion worked and Molly soon forgot about her absent mother and grumpy father, throwing herself enthusiastically into hot cross bun making. They'd just finished sampling two of an earlier batch when Brody's sharp knock at the back door signalled the ogre had arrived to put a stop to the festivities.

"Come in," Carissa called out, wiping her hands and dabbing at Molly's milk moustache, suddenly self-conscious with the effort she'd made earlier with her appearance.

What had she been thinking? The guy was so in love with his dead wife he wore his grief like a badge of honour. Little wonder he didn't notice she existed, apart from being a playmate for his daughter.

"Something smells good." Brody stepped into the kitchen, immediately dwarfing the space with his presence. She'd always loved the sunny yellow walls, the matching floral curtains and the collection of plates in higgledy-piggledy disarray on the wooden dresser of her kitchen, finding the room cosy. With Brody's glowering presence, the room felt claustrophobic.

"We've been baking, Daddy. Want to try one? I made this one 'specially for you." Molly picked up the lumpiest, ugliest bun of the lot, the one Carissa had put aside because it hadn't quite cooked through and the one that happened to be Molly's first try and handed it to her father.

"Thanks, munchkin."

Carissa folded her arms, sat back and grinned. Serve the grouch right. Maybe eating a bit of raw dough would soften him up? As if.

To his credit, Brody didn't flinch, though she watched his Adam's apple bob up and down convulsively as he struggled to swallow a few mouthfuls.

"Am I a good bun maker, Daddy?"

"You're the best, munchkin." Brody managed a tight smile for Molly while sending a glare in Carissa's direction that read "you could've warned me."

Taking pity on the guy, she stood and headed to the fridge. "Would you like some milk to wash some of that bun down? Molly and I have had a glass each, haven't we, sweetie?"

Molly nodded and reached for another of her bun creations which her father wisely refused this time.

"No thanks, Molly. I'll have my milk then it's time for bed, okay?"

"Don't wanna go to bed."

Carissa stopped mid-pour, surprised at Molly's wail. The little girl had been nothing but polite for the last hour and the petulant tone combined with the sulky pout seemed out of character. But what did she know? Perhaps this was a sign of how Molly dealt with her father's demands on a daily basis? And if so, why wasn't he doing something about it?

Handing Brody his milk with a smirk, Carissa knelt down next to Molly. "Sweetie, remember how we talked about growing big and strong earlier? Well, we all need our sleep to do that. I'm tired and I'm going to bed now too."

Thankfully, Molly stood and slipped a hand into her

father's like a meek lamb being led back to the flock. "Okay. Come on, Daddy, time for me to do some growing."

Expecting a smile, a nod, even a slight inclination of the head in gratitude, the flash of annoyance in Brody's dark eyes surprised her.

Where did that come from? She thought she'd done well in diverting a possible tantrum, he acted like she'd rammed ten raw buns down his throat. The guy had a serious attitude problem and she'd had enough of his moodiness. Not to mention the fact he hadn't batted an eyelid in her direction to indicate he noticed her outfit or the trouble she'd gone to with her face.

"You better go," she said, holding open the door and resisting the urge to kick his butt as he walked through it.

"What do you say to Carissa, Molly?"

"Thanks for having me, Carissa," Molly mouthed in a formal parody of manners obviously drummed into her.

"My pleasure, sweetie. You can come over anytime." Carissa sent a pointed glare in Brody's direction, almost daring him to disagree.

Lucky for him, he managed a terse nod, closely followed by, "Thanks for spending time with Molly, Carissa. I appreciate it. Good night."

Was it? She had her doubts.

Five

Brody dropped a light kiss on Molly's forehead, pulled the bedclothes up and stood back, gazing at his daughter in wonder. He'd never tire of the amazement that overcame him at moments like this, when he realised he'd been a part of creating a precious human life. Kids were the best, no matter how much they squawked, played up and turned the world upside down.

And though he'd been the eternal bachelor before Jackie fell pregnant—and had silently cursed his fate at being stuck with a wife and child when he wasn't ready for responsibility—he'd fallen in love with Molly the minute she'd entered the world, red screwed-up face, covered in white gunk, lusty lungs and all.

Though falling in love came at a price, namely fear. Not a day went by that an awful, soul-destroying fear didn't gnaw at his soul, the fear that one day he'd lose his precious daughter too. As much as he'd told himself his fear was irrational, he couldn't shrug it off. Molly was his world. He loved her. It should be simple but it wasn't. The fear complicated everything: fear of losing her, fear of being a lousy father, fear of doing everything right and having her walk out on him anyway when she was old enough to understand everything, particularly the circumstances surrounding her mother's death.

For a cop who'd once won a bravery award, he'd turned into a coward and it didn't sit well with him, not one bit.

Earlier tonight, another fear had snuck under his guard and held him up, making him want to wrestle and overcome it like a would-be assailant. The fear of attraction, of wanting something he couldn't have, had added to his burden.

That loaded moment when Carissa had looked at him with those big blue eyes filled with wonder, her face covered in flour, her hair a messy riot of blonde curls, had acted like a sucker punch to the gut. Then she'd cleaned up and looked even more incredible and smelled like roses, and his concentration had been shot.

For one, irrational second, he'd almost forgotten he was a man with responsibilities, the main one lying in front of him, sleeping peacefully.

Right now, his number one priority was making a better life for Molly, the main reason he'd ditched Sydney and settled in Stockton alongside Molly's maternal great-aunt.

As for anything else, or any*one* else, he didn't need it.

He didn't do involvement.

He didn't do complication.

He'd had enough of both to last him a lifetime.

"I'm having a very bad day," Carissa said, flinging a roll of gift wrapping on the counter, locking the cash register and grabbing the lunch bag Tahnee held out to her.

"That's what I'm here for, Sis. Time to take a load off and tell me all about it."

Opening the bag, Carissa inhaled and shut her eyes in bliss. "Is this a banana and chocolate croissant I smell?"

"Uh-huh. Thought you could use a pick-me-up from the way you snapped at me on the phone earlier."

Carissa grimaced and led the way into the shop's back room. "Sorry about that. You caught me at a bad time."

"Bad time? Bad day? What gives, Sis? Stockton's resident magic lady never has a bad anything."

As Tahnee shrugged out of her denim jacket and hung it on a pixie peg behind the door, Carissa pondered her response. What could she say?

"I'm concerned about a little girl and it's none of my business. And her father Brody Elliott is a grouch and I want to give him a piece of my mind."

Or better yet, how about *"Brody Elliott is a grouch, a social recluse, and a pain in the butt but I kind of like him anyway?"*

Sounded stupid just thinking about it.

"Has this got anything to do with that hottie neighbour of yours?" Tahnee didn't do innocence very well and with that wicked gleam in her eyes, Carissa knew she'd have to tell her sister something, anything, to stop her from delving too deeply into the reason behind her mood today.

"How do you know he's a hottie? You've only ever seen him in a rabbit suit."

Tahnee grinned and licked strawberry frosting from her fingertips as she demolished the last of her cupcake. Michelle's Patisserie made the best cakes and croissants this side of Sydney and they'd been regular patrons since the popular café opened.

"Oh, I've seen him out of that bunny suit, Sis. Well and truly out of it."

Carissa's heart stopped. Did Tahnee mean what she thought she meant?

Tahnee clapped her hands and bounced on her seat. "I knew it! You should see the look on your face. You've got it bad, Sis. Real bad, for big, beautiful Brody."

"I'm going to kill you," Carissa said calmly, taking a mouth-watering bite out of her croissant and wondering if Tahnee was right.

Did she have a wee crush on her brooding neighbour? The guy had done nothing but rub her up the wrong way since she'd first laid eyes on him and he didn't know she existed in the female sense. Apart from a sensational bod and good looks, he'd done nothing to impress her, even if he had lightened up on her spending time with Molly.

So he had one redeeming feature? That didn't make him a guy she could be interested in. By the permanent scowl he wore, far from it.

"Come on, Sis. Spill it." Tahnee leaned forward, her eyes sparkling.

Carissa shrugged. "Nothing to spill. The guy acts like a hermit and I'm just trying to be neighbourly. You know, to get him out of his shell."

At least, she didn't think there was anything to spill. Surely she didn't look like a woman with a crush? She'd never been any good at hiding her emotions, one of the weaknesses her adoptive father had played on repeatedly, making nasty jibes until she cried. When she'd wised up enough not to respond to his cruelty, he found other ways to torment her: like driving away her friends, withholding pocket money, even letting down the tyres on her bike one day so she couldn't get to her part-time job. Ron Lovell had been a creep. In the fatherhood stakes, Brody looked like a saint next to him. Not that she should even compare the two in the same thought.

"I'm so impressed, that sounds downright charitable of

you, taking pity on the man and trying to draw him out." Tahnee rolled her eyes. "Okay, cut to the chase, Sis. You like him, don't you?"

Carissa licked her finger and dabbed at the croissant flakes scattered in the bottom of the bag. "He's a single father doing it tough. Guess I admire him for that."

Tahnee grinned. "Is that all you admire about him?"

Carissa thought about his great body, his melted chocolate eyes and the sexy smile she'd only glimpsed once, before banishing the image from her mind. "He's not bad looking, I guess."

"You're doing an awful lot of guessing. You *guess* you admire him, you *guess* he's not bad looking. If you ask me, I *guess* you have a thing for Mr. Tall, Dark and Dangerous?"

Before Carissa could truthfully answer "damned if I know," the soft tinkle of the front door bell wrested her attention.

"Let me serve this customer and when I get back, I'll set you straight on how inaccurate your guess is," Carissa said, knowing her sister might have a small point but determined to ignore it anyway.

She wasn't interested in a relationship and even if she was, brooding Brody Elliott would be the last man she'd consider.

"Hello? Anyone here?" A loud voice bellowed and Carissa hurried into the shop, fixing a welcoming smile on her face.

As soon as she caught a glimpse of her first customer for the afternoon, she hoped her smile didn't falter. Daisy Smythe had never set foot in *Fey For Fun* even for a browse as most locals had at one time or another, and by the supercilious expression on her wrinkled face devoid of make-up, Carisssa couldn't hazard a guess as to why the old woman had now.

Unless Daisy had heard about her playing with Molly, in which case, she knew her newest customer wasn't here to browse, she was here to interrogate.

"Good afternoon. Can I help you with anything or are you happy to look around?"

From behind blue-rimmed spectacles, Daisy pinned her with an astute stare that travelled from the top of her flyaway curls to her toes poking out from her worn black sandals. "I would like some help."

"Certainly."

"Starting with why you're so interested in spending time with my great-niece."

Carissa gulped at the accusatory glint in Daisy's beady black eyes and wracked her brain for an appropriate answer, fearing whatever she said would fall well and truly short of what Molly's great aunt would want to hear.

"Molly is my neighbour. She's a lovely-natured little girl and I'd like to offer her my friendship."

Daisy pursed her lips, adding to the wrinkles around her mouth and Carissa braced for a lecture. In the old woman's defence, she'd be just as protective if some stranger took a liking to one of her nieces—if she had any.

"Good answer, young lady. Molly can use all the friends she can get and I've heard nothing but praise for you and the way you treat the children in this town. Most of the parents rave about your parties and the pageants you host at Easter and Christmas time. Now, if you can help me choose a birthday present for the young lady in question, I'd be most grateful."

Carissa stood there, gob-smacked, before recovering her wits when Daisy sent her another one of those intimidating glances.

"Molly has been talking nonstop about some fairy movie she saw at your house the other night. Perhaps one of those for a start?"

"Yes," Carissa managed to say, hoping that Molly hadn't told her great-aunt anything else about that night, like how she'd acted like a lunatic when a mouse ran across the kitchen floor. Somehow, she had a feeling Daisy wouldn't be too impressed by anyone showing fear. The old duck probably wasn't scared of anything.

"And perhaps she'd like one of these fairy costumes? Molly would look adorable in one." Carissa held up a pale pink tutu with matching sequinned bodice and gossamer-thin silk wings edged in silver. "When is her birthday?"

"The Sunday after Easter," Daisy said, nodding in approval at the costume. "I'll take it. You have good taste, young lady."

Carissa smiled her thanks and headed for the cash register, thankful she'd escaped any further interrogation about the evening Molly had spent at her house.

However, her relief was short-lived.

"Molly tells me you discussed her mother," Daisy said, rummaging in her handbag for her purse.

"Uh, yes," she mumbled, concentrating on ringing up Daisy's purchases to avoid looking the old woman in the eye. This was beyond awkward.

"My niece's death was a terribly sad business for all involved but thankfully, Molly has coped well. Now, how much do I owe you, dear?"

Dear? Carissa had progressed from 'young lady' to 'dear' in the space of two minutes. She must be doing something right.

"Fifty-two dollars, please. And gift-wrapping is free of charge."

Daisy nodded and handed over the exact money while Carissa reached for the scissors.

"Now, Molly's father is a different matter all together." Daisy made disapproving clucking sounds. "Brody has been mourning for far too long. It's time he had a good woman in his life, someone who would love Molly more than her mother did."

The scissors skewed off the paper and Carissa had to cut a new piece as she studied the gold paper with intense concentration. From the little information Brody had shared at the dinner she'd cooked for him, she was under the impression their marriage had been perfect and they'd lived a charmed life with their daughter? So what was Jackie's aunt doing besmirching the dead woman's memory? And Carissa thought her closet rattled with family skeletons.

"I'm sure Brody will move on when he's ready," Carissa said, laying the scissors down before she spoke. One ruined sheet of the exquisite wrapping was enough for one day.

"Men can be so obtuse," Daisy muttered, shaking her head like a wise old sage. "I'm glad you're spending time with Molly."

Oh no. Somehow, Daisy had deduced that her spending time with Molly meant *she* was the woman for Brody? Uh-uh. Even though she loved Molly, Brody was a different matter. Carissa had enough baggage of her own without getting involved with a guy still in love with his dead wife. She may have made some stupid choices with men in the past but not anymore.

Rather than set the record straight with Daisy and potentially enter a discussion she had no intention of having, she finished wrapping the gifts in record time and handed them over.

"Here you are. I'm sure Molly will love your choices."

"Thank you, dear. With your input, she's sure to enjoy them."

Carissa breathed a sigh of relief as the old lady strode towards the door, her back ramrod straight. She'd escaped relatively unscathed from her encounter with Molly's great-aunt. However, as she tidied the counter and waited for the old woman to leave, Daisy paused at the door.

"Oh. I almost forgot. I'm having a little gathering for

Molly's birthday and I'd like you to come. Next Sunday, five o'clock, at The Grange. Don't be late."

An invitation to the exclusive Grange?

For the second time in as many minutes, Carissa stared at the old lady, gob-smacked.

Six

Brody hated parties. Socialising involved boring small talk, polite smiles and fake exchanges with people he didn't give a hoot about. However, Daisy had gone to a lot of trouble to organise a birthday party for Molly and the least he could do was don his gracious party persona for a few hours.

"Brody, would you mind wheeling the drinks cart into the garden? There are some thirsty kids out there." Daisy picked up a tray of plastic cups and flashed him a smile that made him grumpier before she headed out the door.

He wasn't a fool. The old lady tolerated him because he was Molly's father. Nothing more, nothing less. Though today, for some strange reason he was yet to fathom, she'd been warmer than a summer's day at Bondi, smiling at him, patting his arm, and even straightening his collar at one stage.

His latent cop instincts screamed something wasn't right and the minute he wheeled the cart bearing enough cordial and fizzy drink to ensure hyperactivity in the party-goers for the evening, he knew exactly what it was.

"Hi, Brody," Carissa said, her soft voice delivering an

emotional punch to his gut that had him sucking in air like a diver surfacing.

He'd deliberately avoided her, not willing to tempt fate since that night a spark of attraction had flared between them, though Molly kept him up to date with her regular after-school play time at Carissa's. Apparently, there had been plenty of fairy fun, no more mice and no men. Looked like her Easter bunny had well and truly bounded away, not that he should give a damn.

She could spend time with whoever she chose. His interest was purely for his daughter's sake. He didn't want Molly around strange men, guys he didn't know.

"Hey." His greeting came out sounding like a grunt and her face fell, making him feel like a creep.

But isn't that what he wanted? To push her away before she got any ideas, like that moment when he tucked a curl behind her ear meant something.

"Daisy invited me. Hope you don't mind."

She stood there, uncertainty flickering across her face as she stared at him with those luminous blue eyes and he clenched his hands.

He could do this. Just be polite.

"Daisy can invite anyone she wants. It's her home."

So much for polite. By the flicker of sadness in her eyes, he knew he'd hurt her with his gruff response. .

Softening his tone, he said, "Molly will be thrilled to see you. You're all she talks about these days."

His efforts were rewarded with a small smile. "Really? She's a wonderful child, so bright and enthusiastic. But I guess you already know that, right?"

He nodded, watching Molly play pin-the-tail-on-the-donkey with a dozen of her classmates, the centre of attention and loving it. Yeah, Molly was special all right. So why did it annoy him so much when Carissa pointed it out? Was she implying he couldn't recognise his own daughter's talents?

"I haven't seen you around much. Been busy?"

Busy? He was bored out of his brain now that he'd sanded and painted the house, and trimmed and weeded the garden. It had been a year since he'd quit the force and though he didn't miss it, he wished he could find something satisfying to fill his days. Something other than dwelling in the past and wondering what might have been if he'd thrown the book at the punk who'd killed his wife first time around.

"Yeah, renovations are the pits."

"Molly says you're finished?"

He managed a tight smile, wondering what else his daughter had been telling his neighbour: like how Daddy couldn't sleep most nights, how he found himself staring out the kitchen window at regular intervals in the direction of her house, how he'd be in the garden some mornings, hoping for a glimpse of her blonde curls catching the sunlight as she left for work.

"Yeah, all done. Guess it's time I found a new project to sink my teeth into."

"Anything in mind?" She absentmindedly twirled a curl around her finger and he thrust his hands in his pockets to prevent from reaching out and taking over the action. He'd give anything to wrap that silky golden strand around his finger and gently tug on it until her lips were mere centimetres from his...

"Brody?"

His head snapped up and for one humiliating moment, he wondered if he'd been leaning towards her.

"Not really. Job-wise, there's not much around for a washed-up cop. Interest-wise, nothing has grabbed me."

"Well, if you want to put those handyman skills of yours

to work, I've got plenty of stuff around the shop that needs doing."

Great. If he volunteered to help, he'd be forced to be near her, a dangerous proposition for his wakening libido. If he didn't help, he'd look like a first class jerk. What was it about this woman that tied him up in knots?

"Carissa, you're here!" Molly flew across the lawn and wrapped her arms around Carissa's legs, hanging on tightly.

Brody sent a silent prayer heavenward for his reprieve, even though he had his doubts about the big guy and the power he wielded over his life. After all, look at the mess it had turned out so far. Not that he'd forgotten his bargain the other week for Molly being okay. He'd been trying in the father stakes, he really had. As for being nice to Carissa, guess he had a way to go there.

"Hi, sweetie. Happy birthday." Carissa bent down and hugged Molly, the sight of the two blonde heads so close together affecting him more than he'd like to admit.

The bond between Carissa and Molly had been instantaneous and any fool could see the two had grown amazingly close. Molly's behaviour had improved dramatically since she'd been spending time with his neighbour and he'd noticed subtle changes: the French braids tied in rainbow-coloured ribbons, the new pink lace-topped socks and a delicate bracelet of fairies holding hands that Molly never took off.

Carissa was good for Molly. And good for him, if he ever let go of his guilt and moved on with his life.

"Is that for me?" Molly's eyes grew wide as she spied the huge gold box tied in fairy ribbon behind Carissa.

"Sure is, sweetie. Want to open it now?" Carissa glanced up at him, as if second-guessing she'd done the right thing.

Hell, was he that much of an ogre?

Considering the way he'd been treating her in the hope to push her away, the answer was a no-brainer.

He nodded and managed a smile, her answering grin sending the blood roaring through his veins.

"Oh, boy!" Molly said, ripping the paper with frantic hands, eager to get to the goodies beneath. "This box is humungous."

"I hope you like it," Carissa said, straightening and rubbing a spot in the middle of her back.

A startling impulse to do the same had him questioning everything, as he'd been doing ever since he met this intriguing woman. Was it time to move on with his life? To put the past behind him and take a chance on the future? Molly loved this woman and he knew he could fall for her, given half a chance.

But what if he ultimately lost her? What would that do to Molly? To him? For as long as he could remember, he'd associated love with loss. He'd loved his mum, she died of pneumonia when he'd been ten. He'd loved his dad, he died a few months later of a heart attack—a broken heart, more like it. His uncle Claude, who raised him after his parents' death, had died when he'd been eighteen.

And then there was Jackie.

Could he go through the pain of love again?

"Wow! A doll's house." Molly jumped up and down on the spot, clapping her hands. "I love dolls! Thank you, thank you, thank you, Carissa."

"You're welcome, sweetheart. Your dad can take it home and set it up for you, okay?"

Molly pouted. "But I want to play with it now."

Once again, Carissa looked at him uncertainly.

"Molly, your friends are waiting for you to cut the cake. Why don't I pack all your presents in the car and that way, they'll be ready for you to play with later at home?"

By the mutinous expression on Molly's face, he expected a rebellious tantrum. She hadn't had one in a while but back in Sydney, her erratic behaviour had worried him. He hated giving in to her but if it kept the peace, an often fragile peace, he'd do it.

"That's a great idea," Carissa said, and just like that, Molly smiled and ran away to join her friends.

He should've been ecstatic that a potential scene had been avoided, grateful that Carissa was so good with his daughter. Instead, an irrational petty jealousy filled him that this woman could enter their lives and have such an impact in a short space of time. He'd been trying for years to be a good parent yet Carissa seemed to have more clues than he did.

"That gift is way too extravagant," he said, pointing at the doll's house. "What are you trying to do? Buy her affection?"

Carissa took a step back as if he'd struck her, the hurt in her eyes making him feel like the biggest bastard in the world.

"I thought Molly would enjoy a doll's house. She keeps talking about her dolls all the time."

Running his hand through his hair, he knew he had to make amends for his last comment. He'd been way out of line, his inane jealousy making him more of a social misfit than ever. However, before he could utter a word, she wheeled around and walked away.

"Carissa, wait." He laid a hand on her arm, silently cursing when heat sizzled between them. This wasn't the time to acknowledge his growing attraction to her, it was time to make amends. And fast. She deserved his thanks at the marvellous job she was doing with Molly, not some nasty comeback because he couldn't handle his own insecurities.

She shrugged him off, staring at the spot where he'd held her as if he'd branded her. "If you think that giant chip on your shoulder excuses your rude behaviour, you're wrong. I'm going to spend some time with the kids. At least I might get a civil conversation out of them."

"Look, I'm sorry. You didn't deserve that. Wouldn't you rather stick around here with the grown-ups?"

As far as an apology, it was lousy and he knew it. But he had to start somewhere and hopefully, she'd listen. Not that he'd blame her if she didn't. She was right. He did have a chip on his shoulder and he used it to push everyone away.

He didn't want pity. He didn't want affection. Getting close involved pain and loss and devastation and he couldn't go there. Though maybe, just maybe, having Carissa in his life could change all that.

"Grown ups?" She looked him up and down, wrinkling her nose as if he were the last man on earth she'd want to spend time with. "When you grow up, let me know."

And with that, she headed into the garden where the kids cavorted and trailed after her, reinforcing how popular she was with everyone. And what a low-down grouch he was.

"You've lost your touch, sonny."

He jumped, wishing Daisy wouldn't sneak up on him like that. She'd always done it, even when Jackie was alive, pronouncing her view on the world—usually the opposite of his—as if he was interested.

"My touch?" If he played dumb, perhaps the old bat would leave him alone.

"With the ladies. You've been hiding behind your grief for far too long and it's high time you shrugged it off and move on with your life." She folded her arms and nodded emphatically, almost dislodging her blue-rimmed spectacles in the process.

"Tell me what you really think," he muttered, not in the mood for this lecture. Not that he'd ever be in the mood.

"I usually do, not that you listen," she said, knocking on his head with a bony knuckle. "Mmm, not hollow, which means you have got half a brain in there. When are you going to start using it?"

Daisy pointed at Carissa, currently on all fours with Molly clambering on her back. "See that young lady out there? She's a gem, and what's more, she's crazy about your daughter. And by Molly's constant chatter, the feeling is mutual. So what are you going to do about it?"

He watched Molly shriek with laughter as Carissa bucked like a bronco and his daughter tumbled onto the lawn, taking Carissa with her.

"Just what I'm doing now. Encouraging their friendship."

And working through his own warped feelings. Carissa was a warm, caring woman and the last thing he wanted to do was build false hope. He knew a woman like her would demand it all, one hundred percent emotional commitment, and so she should. She deserved it, for he'd yet to meet anyone with a kinder heart than his neighbour.

However, right now, he could barely offer her ten percent of his screwed up emotions. The icy wall he'd built around his heart years ago may be slightly thawing but it would take time, and courage to face the demons that thaw awakened.

Daisy shook her head and cast him a pitying glance. "Jackie was a rotten wife and mother yet here you are, using her memory to push away a woman who could help heal you and bring joy to your daughter's life."

"I don't want healing."

Not until he was sure he could face all the possibilities that healing would entail, like a possible relationship, a possible reopening of old wounds, a possible letting himself love and be hurt again.

Daisy patted his arm. "No, you don't want healing. You *need* healing. Just don't take too long in making up your mind where Carissa's concerned because I have a feeling a smart girl like her won't wait around forever."

"Daisy, butt out." He glared at Daisy but she merely raised an eyebrow and chuckled.

"Gladly, my boy. Just remember what I said." With one last squeeze on his arm, Daisy walked away to join the party, leaving him with a distinct urge to run like hell.

So the old dame thought he needed healing? Maybe she was right, but it scared the hell out of him.

Following Daisy's footsteps, he plastered a smile on his face and picked up Molly, swinging her high in the air until she squealed with delight.

There was no maybe about it. Daisy *was* right. He needed something in his life, someone to heal the scars, to make him live again.

Until now, he thought he'd had that someone. Molly was all he needed. But what if he needed more?

As for Carissa in his life?

He needed to make up for his Neanderthal behaviour, vowing to show her just how grown up he could be.

Seven

Carissa flipped the open sign to closed and reached for the lock as a shadow darkened the door of *Fey for Fun*.

"Well, well, well. If it isn't Prince Charming," she muttered, switching the lock and glaring at Brody through the glass.

He rattled the doorknob and looked at her in surprise. "Hey, aren't you going to let me in?"

"No."

She folded her arms and gave him her best "don't mess with me" glare, while trying not to notice how incredible he looked in a navy polo shirt and khaki shorts. Then again, she though he looked good in anything.

What was she thinking? She was mad at this guy, madder than she'd ever been with anyone. All she'd done was extend the hand of friendship to him and his gorgeous little girl and he'd treated her badly. She still hadn't forgiven him for his wisecrack about trying to buy Molly's affection and when he'd come knocking on her door after the party yesterday, she'd pretended to be asleep.

If he wanted to apologise, she wouldn't make it easy for him. She was done playing Miss Nice.

"You should let me in. I come bearing gifts."

Her heart kicked at his sexy smile but she shook her head anyway. "No."

"It's food."

"No."

"Chocolate and banana croissants. Your favourite."

Her mouth watered and her stomach rumbled but she held firm. "No."

He held up the bag from *Michelle's Patisserie* and swung it from side to side as if trying to hypnotise her. "Call it a peace offering."

Thankful that the glass shielded the tantalising aromas she knew would be creeping out of the bag, she took a step back. "No. You'll have to do better than that."

"I've got my tool belt in the car. How about I tackle all those odd jobs you need done around here?"

She thought about the loose door hinges, the creaky shutters, the faulty tap washers, and leaky pipe in the back room hand basin—and the croissants in the bag—and reluctantly flicked the lock.

Okay, so the guy didn't play fair. What was a girl supposed to do? She'd always had a thing for tradesmen, finding the whole big, brawny, overall-wearing, tool-belt-slinging, capable man, a major turn on. Combine that little fantasy with the thought of Brody Elliott in a tool belt and well...she was a goner.

Opening the door, she waved him in. "You've said the magic password."

"But I didn't say open sesame?"

"No, you went one better. The words tool belt will get you in every time."

"Oh, really?" He leaned in the doorway, a knowing smirk

THE GRUMPY GUY

on his handsome face and for one crazy moment, she forgot how mad she was supposed to be with him and stifled the urge to haul him into her shop by his lapels, lock the door and create a little magic of her own.

Fighting a rising blush and losing, she swivelled away from him and headed for the back. "I'm starving. Bring your peace offering out here and we'll have a coffee before you get started."

"Long day?" He followed her into the cramped back room and she suddenly wondered at the wisdom of her decision to invite him in.

Dusk had fallen, they were alone in a confined space, and her imagination had taken flight the minute he'd mentioned his tools.

"Uh-huh, definitely one of those days." Busying herself with the cups, she didn't sense him sneaking up on her until it was too late.

"You look tense," he said, reaching around her to place the bag of croissants on the tray she'd arranged, effectively trapping her between his body and the bench.

Heat radiated off him, warming the bare skin on her back. Of all days she had to wear a halter top...

She took a steadying breath, hoping to get her pulse under control before she turned to face him. Instead, the heady combination of warm chocolate, cinnamon and pure Brody assaulted her senses, leaving her more breathless.

And confused. One minute, he was pushing her away using every weapon in his nasty verbal arsenal, the next he was doing his nice act. The guy was driving her mad.

"Here, let me," he said, pouring the boiling water into two mugs and arranging the croissants on a plate.

He was right. She was tense. And getting tenser by the minute with him standing so darn close.

"Thanks," she said, bustling around like a busy bee and

giving him no option but to back off or bump into her. "Sugar?"

"No thanks. I'm sweet enough."

"That's debatable." She handed him a mug, taking care to avoid brushing his fingers.

Tahnee was right. She did have a teensy, weensy crush on this guy, bad attitude and all, and the funny thing was, she could handle him being grumpy but his nice side scared the daylights out of her.

Sipping her coffee, she tried to ascertain his mood by staring at him over the rim of her mug. Their gazes locked across the tiny room and she expected him to look away, to mumble something about getting to work.

He didn't and the moment stretched on forever, a loaded silence fraught with electricity that zapped between them even at this distance.

"Guess I deserved that."

"Yep, you sure did." She picked up a croissant, took a bite and sighed with pleasure. "Mmm...If this is your way of apologising for acting like a jerk yesterday, it's a start."

She expected him to bristle, to glower, to frown. Instead, he managed a rueful chuckle, the sound of his deep laughter warming her better than the Brazilian coffee she was addicted to.

"Hey, can't blame a guy for trying. I thought it was pretty grown up of me to find out your weakness for croissants, and surely with my expertise as a handyman, you can wipe the slate clean?"

"I haven't seen how you wield your tools yet." Darn it, now he'd think she was flirting with him.

He grinned, a wicked grin that spoke volumes. "Ah, but you will. And I guarantee you'll be impressed."

"We'll see." She kept her answer deliberately evasive, one hundred percent cool. No use advertising the fact she was a total schmuck and had a crush on the grizzly from next door. "How did Molly pull up after the party?"

Once again, he smiled and if she'd been counting them, she was sure he'd just created a personal best. She'd never seen him this relaxed and if brooding Brody captured her attention, mellow Brody knocked her for a six.

"She had a ball. I'm happy she's made friends in town so quickly and looks like Daisy is making a big effort to get to know her." His smile faded and he glanced away, not quite meeting her eyes. "Speaking of the party, I really owe you an apology. I was way out of line with that comment about buying Molly's affection. I'm sorry. Guess I'm just not used to sharing her."

"You were jealous?" she asked, wondering what had gotten into the guy. First the record number of smiles, now a genuine apology?

A few men she'd had the misfortune to know had never apologised for anything, especially her adoptive father who would've rather eaten dirt than say the S word. And if anyone should've apologised, it was Ron Lovell.

"Yeah, pretty lame, huh? You've been a great influence on her and don't think I'm not grateful, but it's tough when I've done it on my own for so long and then you waltz in and click with Mol in a second."

Jeez, what could she say to that? The guy had actually said more than two words to her, two nice words that is, and he'd been honest too.

"Molly's a great kid. Anyone would take to her. Apology accepted. Now, how about getting to work? I need to be home by seven." She drained her coffee and rinsed the mug, hoping her brisk response would discourage him from delving into why her mood had soured.

Memories did that to her every time, no matter how positive she tried to be. Losing her parents had been bad enough, being separated from her sisters another devastating blow. And being adopted by the Lovells had capped off the horror stakes.

Sensing her withdrawal, he cast a perplexed look her way. "Hot date, huh?"

"Yeah, something like that."

"I'll be out of your way as soon as I can. Just show me what needs to be done." His smile vanished and the residual tiny frown reappeared between his eyebrows.

"I'm meeting my sister for dinner," she said, wondering what prompted her to explain. She didn't owe him anything and the way he'd been treating her before today, she had every right to be terse.

Tired of mixed messages, tired of tiptoeing on eggshells around this guy and tired of her ridiculous crush, she donned her Caring Carissa cap again, the one that everyone said fitted her so well, and smiled.

"Look, I really appreciate you doing this. Sorry for being grumpy, I'm just tired."

His frown eased and he crossed the room in three strides, laying his mug down on the sink. "Anything I can do?"

Yeah, stop being so darn nice. He was confusing her.

"How about starting with the leaky tap washers in here?"

"Okay."

She expected him to swivel on his heel, head out to the car and grab his tools. Instead, he reached out and tucked a curl behind her ear, the same way she'd seen him do with Molly and inexplicably, tears filled her eyes.

"You're a good woman, Carissa Lewis. I'd like us to be friends."

She would've preferred 'stunning', 'attractive' or 'gorgeous'. However, she'd settle for 'good'. It was a start, the first real overture at friendship he'd made. And isn't that what she wanted, for them to be friends? For her to be a part of Molly's life?

Lost in the dark intensity of his stare, she knew that for now, being friends was good. As for her stupid crush, and her perception that latent heat simmered below the surface of their tenuous relationship, she would deal with it. No use scaring the guy off when he'd finally extended an olive branch. Besides, it was no big deal. She had crushes on lots of good-looking guys. That didn't mean she wanted a relationship with any of them. As if any of the Hollywood hunks she lusted after would look twice at her anyway.

"Friends," she said softly, as if trying the word on for size and enjoying the fit.

"Friends." Brody's gaze dropped to her lips and for one crazy moment, she thought he might kiss her. Instead, he smiled, gave her a half salute and headed out the door.

Eight

A few weeks later, Brody gritted his teeth and smiled at Carissa, holding the opposite end of the skipping rope that Molly happily jumped over as they turned it.

This friends gig was a hell of a lot harder than he'd anticipated. Not that it was Carissa's fault. She made it so damn easy to like her and he enjoyed her company as much as Molly. No, that wasn't the problem.

He'd never had female friends before. In fact, he'd been starved for female company all his life. After his mum had died, his dad had turned into a recluse, pining away for the one true love of his life. Brody hadn't had many significant women in his life, until he'd turned into a total schmuck around Jackie, long enough to let his guard down.

He'd always been a man's man, valuing the straight-talking company of the boys over an occasional beer and the camaraderie of like-minded guys who understood his drive behind being a cop. Jackie had never understood and it had been one of the many things they'd argued about, yet another wedge that had driven them apart.

If it hadn't been for Molly, the one shining light in that relationship, he wondered if he would've bolted.

"Faster, Daddy. Faster, Carissa," Molly said, waving her arms up and down, tucking her legs higher with each jump.

"Sure thing, munchkin," he said, winking at Carissa who grinned back and turned the rope in perfect sync with him.

No, Carissa wasn't the problem. He was. As the protective wall around his heart crumbled, so did his common sense. In opening his heart to new possibilities, he'd expected to feel nervous and gauche. What he hadn't counted on was this... this...*thing* he felt for Carissa. The harder he tried to convince himself she was just friends material, the more he wanted her. He must be going crazy,

"Daddy, you're not doing it right. Look at Carissa."

With pleasure, he thought, taking in her flushed face, mussed blonde curls and full lips smirking at him over Molly's head.

Damn, those lips...he'd been so close to losing the plot and kissing her in the back room of her shop a few weeks ago and had been wondering about it ever since. What her lips would feel like, how they would taste beneath his...

Maybe letting the wall around his heart crumble wasn't such a good idea after all? Perhaps it was time to start shoving a few bricks back in before he lost it completely?

"Molly has a point, Brody. You need to swing more."

Was that a mischievous glint in her luminous blue eyes or was his overactive imagination taking liberty again? Did his nicer-than-nice neighbour even know the meaning of the word swing in its basest sense?

"Perhaps you should show me?" He parried back, sending her a cocky smile designed to tease and see exactly what she was made of.

Though they'd settled into an easygoing friendship, most of their time was spent with Molly doing stuff like this. He'd been careful to avoid one on one contact since the almost-kiss at her shop, needing to take things slow, to evaluate the newly awakened feelings she stirred up within him.

No use ploughing straight into something when he had no idea what that *something* was.

The rope's tempo picked up from Carissa's end, forcing him to match it, much to the squealing delight of his daughter.

"Let me get this straight, Brody. You want me to show you how to swing?" Her smirk widened into a knowing grin, a cheeky sparkle in her eyes.

The little minx was flirting with him, no two ways about it.

"You got it in one. Think you're up for it?"

"I'm up for anything," she said, sending him a sizzling glance from beneath her lashes that could've scorched the rope to cinders if it got caught in the crossfire.

"I'll remind you of that later," he said, with a pointed look at Molly who had stopped jumping and was watching their banter with avid interest.

His daughter was six going on twenty and he didn't want her picking up on the vibes between him and Carissa. She already loved their neighbour and if she sensed that her father had an interest too...No, he wouldn't go there.

His little girl was of the age where she paired off everything from her dolls to her teddy bears and if she turned her attention to him and Carissa...playing make-believe was one thing, giving hope to his precious daughter another.

"Daddy, look. Aunt Daisy is here."

Great, just what he needed, the interfering old biddy to find him in a family-like activity with Carissa. She already had them half way up the aisle in her dotty mind if her none-too-subtle hint at Molly's party had been any indication.

"Aunt Daisy, come and play with us. Daddy and Carissa are real good at it."

"Out of the mouths of babes," Daisy murmured, raising an eyebrow as she stared at him over her spectacles.

To his annoyance, heat crept into his cheeks as if she'd caught them in a compromising situation rather than playing skipping rope with Molly.

"What brings you by, Daisy?" Whatever it was, he hoped it wouldn't take long so she could hop back in her car and take her prying eyes with her.

Waving at Carissa, Daisy bent down to Molly's height with surprising agility for a woman her age. "Actually, I need Molly's help. How would you like to come to my house and help me bake choc chip cookies? I need to make several dozen for the church fair this weekend so I need my official cookie apprentice on hand."

Molly's eyes lit up as her gaze swung to his. "Can I, Dad? I love making cookies almost as much as skipping."

Brody scanned Daisy's face, looking for an ulterior motive. Was this an attempt at matchmaking on the old woman's part? Or was she genuinely interested in indulging Molly? Either way, it would leave him alone with Carissa and maybe it was time to knock down a few more of those bricks?

"I can vouch for Molly's cookie making skills," Carissa chimed in. "She's a real champion at it. Especially licking the spoon." Carissa winked at Molly, who promptly broke into giggles.

Torn between wanting to sweep Molly into his arms for protection against the two women who seemed to be ganging up on him, and spending some adult time with Carissa—and seeing exactly how far she was willing to take their flirting—he hid behind his usual taciturn self when confronted by indecision.

"Fine," he bit out. "Just don't eat too much, Molly. You'll spoil your dinner."

Daisy's smile screamed victory, reinforcing his earlier suspicion he'd been duped. "Oh, don't worry about that. I've already whipped up Molly's favourite, so she can stay for dinner too."

Before he could open his mouth to refuse, Molly said, "Spaghetti? Really? I love spaghetti. But not as much as cookies," she added as an afterthought, obviously fearing she'd lose out on the cookies.

Reluctant to put a dampener on Molly's enthusiasm and grateful that his daughter had blossomed under the tutelage of her great-aunt, he nodded. "Okay, you can stay for dinner too. I'll pick you up at eight."

"Thanks, Daddy."

He bent down so Molly could plant one of her trademark sloppy kisses on his cheek and cuddled her close, knowing he wouldn't have this luxury forever. All too soon his little girl would grow up and deem it 'uncool' to cuddle her father. He wasn't looking forward to that day one bit.

"Be good, munchkin."

She giggled into his shoulder. "I'm always good, Daddy."

"Grrr," he growled, picked her up and swung her around while she squealed with laughter. Setting her back on the ground, he tapped her lightly on the nose and said, "See you later."

"I can bring Molly home if you'd like," Daisy volunteered, taking hold of Molly's hand and waving at Carissa, who hadn't said much since the old woman arrived. "It's no trouble. I'm sure you could use the time to yourselves," Daisy continued, her beady gaze shifting between the two of them as if trying to figure out what was going on between them.

Yeah, no doubt about it. She'd said 'yourselves' which

meant she hoped he'd spend his free time with Carissa. The meddling old busybody...

Well, if Daisy wanted something to stew over, he'd give it to her. Might keep her off his case for a while.

"Fine. Thanks Daisy. I could use the time, especially as Carissa is going to teach me how to swing."

"Swing?" Daisy's eyebrows shot upwards, almost hidden by her grey fringe, as the corners of her mouth twitched like a rabbit picking up the scent of a juicy carrot.

"It's a type of dance," Carissa blurted, her cheeks almost matching her scarlet tank top.

"Is it really?" Daisy's smile spoke volumes as she tugged on Molly's hand. "Come on, Molly. Let's go bake some cookies."

He winked at Carissa and she poked her tongue out, her colour deepening as he returned the gesture.

"Enjoy your dancing," Daisy called out from the car while Molly waved through the windscreen. "Bye Dad. Bye Carissa. Keep playing if you want."

As the car pulled out of the drive, he crossed the lawn to stand by Carissa as she said, "So, do you want to keep playing?"

Chapter 9

Carissa knew her cheeks blazed with colour. She could feel the heat seeping from her neck upwards, a shining beacon to her nerves.

So she'd flirted a little? Where was the harm in that? She'd flirted with plenty of men before.

Yeah, boring men. Safe men, men who didn't challenge her. Or intrigue her.

And unfortunately, Brody Elliott did both.

She'd expected him to revert to casual friend mode as soon as Daisy left with Molly. And she was right.

"Guess I'll leave you to it," he said, ignoring her question and casting a longing look in the direction of his house. "I've got loads to do and I'm sure you have too."

She shouldn't flirt with him. She really shouldn't, but a little demon had lodged in her brain and wouldn't stop prodding her with its loaded pitchfork.

"Actually, I don't have much to do. Maybe you still want to play?" she asked, leaning against the wrought-iron outdoor table in a provocative pose designed to tease.

"Uh, no," he mumbled, looking delightfully flustered and she bit back a grin, enjoying this more than she should.

The guy had loosened up a lot over the last month and she enjoyed the easy friendship they'd developed between them. However, that didn't mean she couldn't have a little fun at his expense.

Besides, he looked too damn delectable for her not to tease him on this all-round glorious autumn day: ruffled dark hair, chocolate eyes that bore into her soul, and a sexy smile designed to charm the pants off any woman who didn't know better.

"Have to wash your hair, huh?"

A smile tugged at the corners of his mouth. "Yeah, something like that."

His smile faded as he caught on to the speculative gleam in her eyes.

"You're running scared," she said, taking a step toward him.

"Scared of what?" He backed away.

"This." She took another step forward and poked him in the chest, expecting him to make a run for the house at the brief physical contact.

However, he didn't move a muscle, his dark gaze unreadable, and her pulse accelerated madly as she stood there, lost in his stare.

"And this." She reached up and ran a finger down his cheek, enjoying the rasp of stubble against her fingertip, wondering what it would feel like rubbing over her smooth skin.

Before she had time to think, he grabbed her hand and lowered it, regret mingled with something more, something she could almost label as desire in his fathomless eyes.

"I'm not scared, just wary," he said, taking a step back and looking ready to bolt. "Playing with fire could result in burns."

"Are you referring to me or you?"

He shrugged, the deep crinkle between his brows returning and she wished for just one minute, he'd cast aside his grief and face up to reality. They were two friends having fun, flirting, teasing. It didn't have to get serious. She didn't want that.

What she did want was for this guy to lighten up, to bring him out of his shell, to make him laugh for more than half a second, to bring a smile to his face, the one that made her knees wobble just a tad.

"Maybe both of us." The crinkle deepened and she knew he'd end up lecturing her so she pre-empted it.

"Look, Brody. We're friends and sometimes friends have a little fun. You're locked up in your house most of the time, you don't socialise, you don't go out, you don't do much of anything."

"And you think by touching me I'll change, is that it?"

He had her there. What could she say? That touching his cheek had been a spur of the moment thing, something to make him react when most of the time he acted like she wasn't around except as a playmate for Molly?

"Just forget it," she muttered, thrusting her hands into her jeans pockets like a child who'd been told to pick up their bat and ball and go home.

"I know what you're trying to do," he said, fixing her with that all-seeing stare, the one that made her want to run and hide, the one that seemed to peer into her soul and probe her darkest secrets. "And for what it's worth, thanks. You're a good friend, but I'm not the type of guy to step out of his comfort zone and right now, I'm comfortable. I have Molly and that's more than any man could wish for in a lifetime."

Carissa's breath caught and she swallowed the lump of emotion in her throat. Jeez, when this guy opened up, he didn't do it by halves. His honesty left her wanting to touch him more than ever, to cradle him in her arms and never let go. He was hurting, that much was obvious, and coaxing him out of his safe cocoon could surely benefit him.

"I understand," she said, hoping her voice wouldn't waver and grateful when it didn't. "Sorry if I came on a bit strong."

"You didn't. It's just been a while since I've done the whole flirting thing. Guess I'm lousy at it."

Awww…this softer Brody was too much.

"How about we have coffee and brownies that I baked earlier? And I promise not to flirt too much. Deal?"

He smiled but the wary expression hadn't left his eyes, as if he half expected her to jump him. Sheesh. And she thought she didn't get out much.

"Deal. Your place or mine?"

Her eyes flew to his and sure enough, there was a twinkle there.

"Mine. And careful there, Mr. Elliott, that almost bordered on flirting."

"Must be your bad influence. Shall we?" He offered her his arm and she laid a hand on it, joining in his laughter as they headed over to her place.

Maybe there was hope for him yet?

Chapter 10

Brody waited until the scattered applause died down before waving to the kids and beating a hasty retreat to the back of the classroom.

"Thanks, Mr. Elliott. Your talk about the police force was very informative. Hopefully we'll see you here for the next career's day?" Mrs. Hanratty, the eighth grade teacher at Stockton High, fixed him with a determined glare that meant she wouldn't take no for an answer.

Brody managed a tight smile which must've come out more a grimace as a few kids in the front row tittered and he quickly slipped out of the classroom, breathing a sigh of relief.

He'd kill Daisy. Lately, she'd lined up a whole host of 'activities' for him on the pretext of keeping him occupied. But he knew better. The old woman was onto him and far too canny for her own good.

It had been a year since he'd quit the force and two months since he'd settled in Stockton, enjoying his 'time out'. He'd spent the last ten years doing right by other people, protecting and serving the community, and felt entitled to a little down time.

However, now that Molly had settled into her new school and he'd made a home for them, it was time to do something with his life. And of course, Daisy had picked up on it.

Speak of the devil...

"Oh, my aching bunions. Canteen duty for a horde of ravenous teenagers is hard work. So, how did it go? Any budding law enforcement officers among that lot?" Daisy asked, linking her arm with his as they headed out to his car.

"Doubt it. Half were asleep while the other half doodled or texted naughty emojis to each other."

Though that wasn't entirely true. His attention had been repeatedly drawn to a young guy in the second last row who had hung on his every word, and he'd seen the avid gleam of ambition in his eyes.

That kid had spunk and though he'd slouched at the end and pretended not to care like the rest of his teenage mates, Brody knew the force had one potential recruit in the wings. In fact, the kid had reminded him of himself at that age: eager, passionate, with a drive to take on the bad guys and win.

Though facing up to causing Jackie's death, he knew firsthand you couldn't win them all.

"Have you given further thought to my other proposal?" Daisy waited until he opened the passenger car door, her expression similar to formidable Mrs. Hanratty's minutes earlier.

"Anyone ever tell you to keep that sticky beak of yours out of other people's business?" He waited until she buckled up before turning the key in the ignition.

"All the time. Now, answer the question, young man."

He checked his side mirror before pulling into the quiet street and heading for The Grange. Not only had he given thought to Daisy's proposal, he'd taken the idea on board and had started planning already. Truth be known, he'd been excited at the prospect of returning to the workforce and though he wouldn't be saving the world this time around, he'd be doing something worthwhile without the added pressure.

Yeah, Daisy had hit the jackpot with her suggestion. Not that he'd tell her. Let the old busybody sweat for a while.

"It's not a bad idea. And I've done a bit of work with troubled teens in Sydney so maybe running a half way house for local kids is worth considering."

"It's more than worth considering. You'd be perfect for the job. Give you something to focus on and get you out of the house at the same time." Her tone had softened and Brody knew that though she presented a tough exterior to the world, Daisy had a heart of gold.

"Leave it with me," he said, biting back a grin.

It wouldn't do him any good to show Daisy he was going soft. She'd take advantage in a second and probably have him lined up to read at the retirement village, walk little old ladies across the main street, and baking for the church fete lamington drive, before he could blink.

"Molly seems to have settled in well"

"Thanks to you." He cleared his throat, finding it difficult to shun his usual reticence and actually have a conversation with the woman who'd made their transition to Stockton smoother than he'd anticipated. "You've been great with Molly and I really appreciate it, Daisy. Moving here is the best thing I could've done for her."

Though he kept his eyes on the road, he sensed the older woman smile. "And what about you, young man? What's the best thing for you?"

"That's easy. Making Molly happy."

Years ago, before he met Jackie, he would've said surfing on the weekends, hanging out with his mates, and being the best damn cop Sydney had ever seen. Funny how life turned out.

"She won't always be a little girl, Brody. What then?"

"I'll face that when I come to it. Besides, I've got years of reading bedtime stories and plaiting pigtails before then."

Years in which to make it up to Molly for leaving her motherless thanks to his stupidity.

"I know my niece wasn't the easiest woman to live with. Don't let your time with Jackie taint what you could have with another woman."

Though Daisy hadn't spelled it out, he knew she meant Carissa. His nosy neighbour had been just that lately: nosy. Always trying to get him to join in the fun with Molly, trying to invite him over for dinner, trying to make him laugh with her natural exuberance. She'd even flirted and touched him to get a reaction. If only she knew exactly how he'd reacted. Parts of him had stirred, parts that hadn't stirred in a long time courtesy of a long neglected libido. In the past, he would've shrugged off his response as hormones but this time, he wondered if a few more of those protective bricks around his heart were crumbling?

If it had been anyone else pushing him like this, he would've told them to leave him the hell alone a long time ago, but the woman was good for Molly and if he was completely honest with himself, she'd made him drop his angry act several times. And on those rare occasions, he'd actually enjoyed himself, though he'd refused most of her invitations apart from the occasional cup of coffee. Besides, she made the best damn brownies this side of Sydney and no man could resist that.

"I'm not ready for another relationship. Don't think I'll ever be." He'd become a crusty old bachelor at the age of thirty two and which woman would be silly enough to take him on?

"You will be when you stop running away from your demons."

So Daisy had guessed that settling in Stockton wasn't just about Molly. The woman was cannier than he gave her credit for. He'd wanted a fresh start, a new beginning to come to terms with the ever-present guilt that gnawed at his soul, in the hope that one day perhaps he could put the past behind him. And if he were honest with himself, so far things were working out better than he'd hoped.

Molly was well-adjusted and happier than he'd ever seen her. As for him, on those rare occasions when he allowed himself to laugh at one of Carissa's corny jokes or caught the cheeky glint in her sky-blue eyes, he almost felt like a man again. A man without guilt tethering him to a past he wished he could change every day. A man with hope for the future, no matter how nebulous it seemed right now.

"And on that note, here we are."

He pulled into Daisy's driveway with a sigh of relief, wanting nothing more than to head home, have a quiet dinner with his daughter, play a few hands of Go Fish and watch his rugby team demolish the opposition on TV once Molly had gone to bed. Though Daisy had the best intentions, he'd had enough of her psychoanalysis for one day.

The old woman turned to him and looked ready to deliver another sermon, so he pre-empted. "Thanks for the half-way house idea. You're a gem. An interfering old gem but a gem all the same."

"Cheeky brute. See you and Molly for dinner tomorrow night."

She closed the car door with a resounding bang and his head lolled against the headrest for a brief moment, wondering if Daisy was right.

What would happen if stopped trying to outrun his demons?

Chapter 11

"There you go, Sweetie. You look like a princess." Carissa slid a pink bow into Molly's curls which hung in soft waves to her shoulders, and dropped a kiss on her head.

"Do you really think so?" Molly twirled in front of the mirror, checking out all angles like a true princess in the making.

"I know so." Carissa plopped onto the floor at Molly's feet and hugged her knees to her chest, feeling like a proud mum watching her little girl preen before a party.

Betty Lovell had never helped her dress and never bought her treats like the small gifts she chose for Molly, a new doll's outfit here, a hair clip there. For Carissa, it wasn't about the gifts so much as the joy of giving them to Molly and seeing the delight light up her face. And the accompanying hug which made her feel like the luckiest woman on the planet.

"Do you know how I know?"

"How?"

"Because I have all sorts of princesses in my shop and you look just like them. Very pretty and ready for the ball."

Molly giggled and sat down next to her. "But I'm not going to a ball. I'm going to Aunt Daisy's for dinner."

"Oh, that's right." Carissa clicked her fingers in an exaggerated response. "I forgot."

"You're funny, Carissa." Molly's giggles intensified and she rested her head against Carissa's shoulder while picking up her favourite doll Pansy, a raggedy cotton thing with a loose arm and a skewed leg. "I like it when you come over and play."

"Me too, sweetie. Me too."

Thankfully, Brody seemed content these days to let her spend as much time with Molly as the little girl liked. She thought she might've blown it last week when she'd taken her teasing a tad far and stroked his cheek but they'd moved past it and their friendship, tenuous as it may be, appeared to be moving forward, albeit at a snail's pace.

"If I'm a princess, does that make daddy a prince?"

Carissa chuckled. "Uh-huh."

Molly paused for two seconds, digesting this latest bit of information, before saying, "Maybe he's Prince Charming?"

Unlikely, Carissa thought. At least, not in her version of the fairytale. Prince Charming needed to live up to the second part of his name and as far as she could see, Brody was anything but. The guy didn't have a sweet-talking bone in his buffed body.

"And if he's Prince Charming, that would make mummy Sleeping Beauty and maybe that's why she's in heaven. She's sleeping and waiting for daddy to go up there and give her a kiss to wake up."

Carissa's heart clenched with sadness at what Molly must go through on a daily basis, wondering why her mum wasn't with her. However, the sadness was soon replaced by something stronger, a righteous anger that Brody needed to explain the situation better to his daughter rather than leaving her to make up stories to satisfy her curiosity.

He wasn't doing Molly any favours by sugar-coating the absence of his wife. If anything, Molly's insecurities would only fester and manifest in some other way. From what she could see, Brody adored Molly, so why couldn't he see what was happening?

"Your daddy and mummy love you very much, sweetie. Always remember that. Now, how about we put your shoes on and see if your dad's ready?"

Thankfully, Molly was satisfied with Carissa's response and jumped to her feet. "Okay. I want to wear the black shiny ones."

"You got it, kiddo."

As Molly stepped into her Mary Janes and Carissa slid the patent leather strap through the buckle, she vowed to mention something to Brody about Molly's constant references to her mother. Burying the truth wouldn't benefit either of them, though she had a feeling that if Brody couldn't face up to the loss of his wife, how on earth would he explain it to his daughter?

"Thanks Carissa. You're the best." Molly flung her arms around her neck and Carissa snuggled into her, inhaling the sweet scent of raspberry bubble bath on Molly's baby-smooth skin.

She loved this little girl and it had nothing to do with seeing herself in Molly at this age: curious, questioning, wanting answers in a world that had none. No, it had more to do with Molly's openness, her capacity to give and receive affection, and her cute personality that would slay anyone lucky enough to know her.

"I think you're the best," Carissa said, pulling back and dropping a kiss on Molly's cheek. "Now, let's go find your dad."

"You don't have to. I'm right here." Brody stepped into the room, his gut twisted in knots.

He'd been standing there long enough to hear Carissa tell Molly how much he and Jackie loved her. Well, she had that right but it was the way Carissa had said it, the patience she'd shown in doing up Molly's shoes, the way she'd embraced his daughter, that him wanting to sweep her into his arms.

How could any man resist a woman treating Molly as if she were her own? In fact, better. Carissa had more of a bond with Molly in a few short months than Jackie had shown in the first few years of Molly's life.

And right then and there, another few bricks around his heart fell.

"Daddy, I'm ready. Look, I've got a bow in my hair."

He dropped a kiss on the bow and ruffled his daughter's loose curls. "I can see that, munchkin. You look gorgeous."

"Carissa said I look like a princess."

"Carissa's right." He winked at her over Molly's head and her answering smile nudged another brick or ten loose.

"Let's go. I'm starving. Maybe Aunt Daisy has cooked 'sketti again. I love 'sketti." Molly tugged on his hand and hopped from one foot to the other.

"Guess that's my cue to leave." Carissa unfolded her denim-clad legs from the floor, the simple action of dusting off her butt pulling her faded blue T-shirt taut across her chest and making his mouth go dry in the process.

Damn, this felt awkward. She'd spent the last hour with Molly, she'd bathed her, helped her get dressed, and now he had to kick her out? He should invite her to dinner but that would give Daisy all sorts of crazy ideas and hot on the heels of their conversation in the car the other day, he didn't want to do that.

Unless he had dinner with her some other night? As a

thank you for all she'd done for Molly. Yeah, that sounded like a plan.

"Molly, would you mind getting my jacket? It's on my bed."

"Sure thing, daddy." Molly scampered off, leaving him to ask out a woman for the first time in seven years.

"Okey, dokey. I'll be off." Carissa smiled and made to move past him but he laid a hand on her arm.

"Carissa, wait."

"Yes?" She stared up at him, curiosity in her blue eyes.

Damn, this would've been easier if she'd been on the other side of the room, not close enough that he could see the gold flecks around her irises or smell the faintest rose essence from her skin.

Electricity arced between them and he wondered if dinner was such a good idea after all. It was one thing to say thank you but what if she stared at him like this, made him laugh like she usually did, and he dropped his guard all together? The results could be cataclysmic.

"Have dinner with me," he blurted, knowing if he didn't get the words out now, he never would.

"Uh...dinner." Her eyes widened slightly as shock replaced the curiosity he'd glimpsed seconds ago.

He rushed on, "Not tonight. Another time, when it's just you and me. As a thank you for all you've done with Molly."

Great, now he was blabbering like an idiot.

"I don't need thanks. She's a special little girl and I love spending time with her."

"Humour me," he said, wondering if he sounded as desperate as he felt. It was his first overture to a woman in years and he doubted if his meagre confidence could stand a knock-back.

How ironic that the cocky guy he'd been in his younger days, the same guy who'd had women slipping their phone numbers into his pocket on a regular basis since he'd turned eighteen, could be this hung up over an invitation to dinner.

Her lips curved into a coy smile. "Are you asking me on a date?"

"It's dinner," he said, not needing the added pressure of putting a label on their dinner together. Date? The mere mention of the word would have him running for the safety of his work shed and not coming out for a week.

"Dinner, huh?" The corners of her lush mouth twitched as if she was laughing at him and strangely enough, he didn't mind.

At one time, he would've walked away without a backward glance—after a scathing word or two—but he'd mellowed recently. And though he had a long way to go to completely let go of his guilt, not beating himself up over Jackie's death on a daily basis was having positive results already.

"Yeah, dinner. You do have to eat at some stage, don't you?"

She paused, looked down at his hand still resting on her arm, which he dropped in record time, before meeting his gaze again, her cheeky grin giving him his answer before she spoke.

"Wow. When you put it like that, how can a girl refuse?"

And with that, she sent him a saucy wave and sauntered down the hallway and out his front door.

Chapter 12

Carissa paced the floor in her living room, smoothing non-existent wrinkles from her dress for the hundredth time since she'd slipped it on. Brody had said dress up for dinner so she'd worn her favourite royal blue sheath which made the most of her limited curves, the thin shoe-string straps leaving her shoulders bare. She'd dusted her upper body in a barely-there layer of bronze powder, adding a sparkle that captured the light when she moved.

With her blonde curls secured in a diamanté barrette, matching drop earrings, and enough make-up to hide the freckles on her nose and illuminate her eyes, she'd donned a confident mask that would hold her in good stead to face the evening ahead. She hoped.

Brody's invitation had floored her. And as much as she'd drummed it into her head that he only wanted to thank her for the time she spent with Molly, she couldn't help but feel a tiny bit flattered that maybe, just maybe, he'd finally noticed her as a woman and not just a playmate for Molly.

The doorbell rang and she jumped, hoping her nerves would settle. Besides, what did she have to be nervous about?

Brody had made it clear. This wasn't a date. It was dinner. The simple act of two people sharing a meal. In a restaurant. At a cosy table. Making conversation. Staring at each other. Smiling. His sexy smile. Yikes.

So much for settling her nerves.

"Breathe, you fool," she muttered, grabbing her evening purse, flicking the lamp on and pasting a smile on her face before she opened the door.

"Hey, Brody." Heat crept into her cheeks as she drunk in the sight of her neighbour sporting a new haircut that shaved years off him, formal black pants, and a snowy white open-necked shirt that accentuated his tan.

The guy was serious drool material. Some friend he was turning out to be. For a girl who didn't want to consider the remotest possibility of a relationship, having her buddy turn up on her doorstep looking like every woman's fantasy come to life wasn't helping matters.

"You look great," he said, his gaze travelling from her bare shoulders to her crimson toenails she'd managed to paint in thirty seconds after her shower and back, appreciation lighting his eyes as dusk descended.

"Thanks. Where are we going?"

"Stockton's finest. The new and improved Kangaroo Corner."

"I haven't been there since it reopened. Tahnee said it's fabulous, with authentic bush tucker food."

"So I hear."

Their conversation came to an abrupt halt and Carissa wondered if Brody had the jitters too. By his general disposition, she doubted he'd dated much since Jackie's death though what did she know? He might have a host of women on standby in Sydney.

Remembering the way he'd asked her out and his lack of response to her flirting, maybe not.

"Come on. We've got a long way to go."

"Yeah, that ten minute walk at a snail's pace is going to be a killer," she said, hoping she'd manage in fancy three inch heels. She never wore dressy shoes as a rule, preferring comfort over style but in this dress and with her height, she needed all the help she could get.

As she teetered down the path next to him, he glanced at her shoes and said, "We could drive, you know."

"And ruin my chance to impress you with my prowess on stilts?"

He chuckled, the deep, rich sound warming her and she wished he would do it more often. Sure, she'd seen him smile a few times now but he didn't laugh very often. In fact, she'd never seen him laugh around Molly either, which was sad. Hopefully, tonight was a step in the right direction for him.

After all her efforts to drag him out of hermitsville, he'd finally surprised her and come out to play.

"Those things do look a bit tricky. My vote would still be for the car. Wouldn't want you twisting an ankle on the way and missing out on an evening of scintillating conversation and wit."

Carissa gaped at him. Not only was he going out, he was poking fun at himself too. Amazing.

"Okay, you've convinced me. The car it is."

"Good. Think you can make it to my driveway in those things?"

"Watch me."

Unfortunately, he did and having her knees quiver at the intensity of his stare didn't help her balancing act as she negotiated cracks in the footpath, a clump of grass, and a carpet of gum-nuts scattered across the lawn.

She reached his car, a newish family sedan, without mishap, and leaned against the passenger door in relief. "There. Nothing to it."

Shaking his head and grinning, he opened the door for her. "Why do women wear those things anyway? They look lethal."

"You wouldn't understand. It's a girl thing. As for lethal, you haven't seen me when I'm starving so let's see what this baby can do. And make it snappy." She tapped the top of the car and slid into the seat, making sure her dress behaved and didn't ride up her legs. No use scaring the poor guy before they even made it to the restaurant.

Rather than laugh, pain flashed across his face and she stared at him in confusion, wondering what she'd said. Maybe it was a cop thing not to make jokes about speeding? She rarely drove these days, preferring the short walk to the shop than getting behind the wheel of her snazzy second-hand sports car but the odd time she'd driven to Sydney with Tahnee she'd been called Lead-foot Lewis.

Better not to let Brody in on that little secret if the mere mention of speed brought on his old grumpy face.

Sliding behind the wheel, he buckled up, glanced across to make sure she'd done the same before turning the ignition. He didn't say a word and she watched him, fascinated by his serious expression and the routine he went through: test tension of seat belt, look in rear vision mirror, check side mirror, glance over shoulder to blind spot, pull away from the kerb at a snail's pace.

She'd never seen anyone drive like that, going through the motions like it was a ritual, and once again she attributed it to a cop thing. Funny, seeing as some of the police she saw driving on the highways appeared to be speeding more than the average motorist.

Thankfully, the drive was quick—she couldn't stand the oppressive silence as all his concentration focussed on the road —and in two minutes, he parked outside Stockton's fanciest restaurant. Kangaroo Corner might have a dinky name but that's where the funny stuff ended. Run by one of Sydney's top chefs who'd defected to Stockton after marrying a local, the food here was legendary. And pricey, which is why she hadn't been since it reopened. Pete had been stingy along with boring and safe.

Opening her door, he smiled and offered her a hand and as she took it, trying not to wobble on her heels, she wondered if she'd imagined the tension of the last few minutes.

"Let's hop right in."

Holding her sides, she faked a laugh. "Stop it. You're killing me."

"Bet you thought tonight would be boring. I'm just trying to impress you with my wit." He guided her up the steps, his hand warm and solid at her elbow.

She sent him a mock frown, then spoiled the affect by collapsing into giggles. "Don't try so hard. I can't take much more of that funny business."

"Lady, if you think that's funny business, you get out even less than I do."

With that cryptic comment, he ushered her into the restaurant where Mandy Morrell, the chef's wife and daughter of Stockton's richest landowner, showed them to their table.

"Have a good evening, folks," Mandy said, winking at Carissa over Brody's head and giving her the universal two thumbs up sign of encouragement.

This isn't what you think, Carissa wanted to say. It had been a long time since she'd had dinner with a man without trying to impress him, or wonder whether he was potential boyfriend material, or silently debating whether she'd let him kiss her at the end of the night. Being here with Brody felt comfortable, felt right, and being friends with a guy was a lot less complicated than the dramas of being in a relationship.

As long as she kept it that way and didn't keep noticing the way his eyes crinkled in the corners when he smiled, or the way his shirt stretched across his broad chest, or the way his sexy smile made her heart trip…

Snapping the menu shut, he said, "I know what I'm having. How about you?"

"Uh, yeah, right," she mumbled, totally sprung. She should've been perusing main courses, not daydreaming about her *friend's* attributes. "I'll have the satays," she said, choosing the first thing her gaze lighted on.

"Interesting choice," he said, a smile hovering around his lips as he turned to the waitress. "I'll have the pan fried kangaroo steaks in port wine sauce please. And a bottle of your finest shiraz."

Breathing a sigh of relief that she'd fluffed her way through that, she handed the menu to the waitress and settled back to enjoy the evening.

"Bet Molly's having a ball at Daisy's," she said, toying with her napkin which had tiny emus printed around the edges. "She couldn't stop talking about the dinner party Daisy had planned for her and Jessie, her best friend."

Brody paused to sniff the wine that had been decanted before nodding his approval for the waitress to pour. "Must admit, I'm relieved the two of them have bonded so quickly. When I first met Daisy, she was a dour old thing who rarely cracked a smile. These days, she's a real trooper."

"Sounds like someone else I know," she mumbled behind her wine glass, taking a sip and savouring the full-bodied ripe flavours of the shiraz against her palate.

"What was that?"

"Nothing." She smiled and lowered her glass. "Why don't you propose a toast?"

"Toast?" The deep crinkle between his brows reappeared as if she'd asked him to translate the menu into Japanese rather than say a few simple words.

"Okay, here's to being friends and the best damn neighbour a guy could wish for." He raised his glass in her direction and she leaned across to clink it. "And thanks for spending so much time with Molly. I'd pay a fortune trying to find a nanny to do half of what you do with her."

And just like that, Carissa's little bubble of self-delusion burst.

Brody didn't see her as a woman. He still considered her a playmate for Molly, someone he could rely on to pick up the slack with his daughter. And speaking of which, she had to approach him about Molly's thoughts on her mother though how she'd introduce that particular topic, she had no idea.

"No worries," she said, faking a smile and breathing a sigh of relief when their meals arrived in record time.

"Mmm, these look good." She concentrated on the food, finding it infinitely easier than maintaining eye contact with the guy whose smile undermined her last thought about him not seeing her as a woman.

"Delish." The peanut sauce added a piquant flavour to the chicken which had been grilled to perfection and she'd shovelled white meat from three out of the four sticks into her mouth before realising she probably looked like a pig.

"Glad you're enjoying it. Must say, I didn't think you'd be that adventurous."

"Hmm?" She finished the last of the satay sticks and mopped up the delicious sauce with a piece of damper bread.

"Choosing a dish like that."

"Satays? What's so adventurous about that?"

The corners of his eyes creased into delightful laugh lines as he grinned. "Tell me you read the fine print under each main."

Fine print? Uh, not likely, seeing as she'd been too busy thinking about his sexy smile at the time.

She shook her head. "I'm pretty decisive when it comes to food. I know what I like and I go for it."

"Oh, so you've tried witchetty grubs before?"

"What?"

He had to be kidding, right? Grubs? She'd eaten grubs?

His grin waned but she could tell he wanted to laugh by the way his mouth twitched. "Apparently they taste just like chicken, so I'm told."

"And who told you that, Mr. Bush Tucker Man?"

Her stomach churned at the thought of grubs crawling around in there before she silently chastised herself to stop being so silly. Her meal had been delicious and *had* tasted like chicken, so much so she'd thought she'd been eating fowl rather than the crawly things fowls ate.

"I read it in the fine print." He burst out laughing and she tried a frown for two seconds before joining in.

Holding her hand up, she said, "Okay, you've had your fun. Why don't you finish that kangaroo steak before it hops off your plate and let me focus on dessert. Surely I can't go wrong there?"

He continued to chortle and picked up his knife and fork, slicing into the rare meat that made her stomach turn more than the thought of the grubs.

"And this time, I'll read the fine print."

She checked out the specials board and decided that quandong soufflé sounded superb—after reading that quandongs were the outback's most famous fruit, a tart peach which grew wild in the desert.

"Good idea." He finished his meal, sipped at his wine and studied her over the rim. "You know, we've been neighbours for a few months now but I don't really know much about you."

Huh? Stockton's resident hermit wanted to get personal? This night was turning into one surprise after another.

She kept her answer deliberately light-hearted, unwilling to spoil the evening with anything too heavy. Besides, she had a feeling she'd be doing that in the not too distant future once she broached the subject of Molly with him.

"What's there to know? I'm a city girl who grew up in Sydney, my adoptive parents died within a year of each other when I was nineteen, Kristen, Tahnee and I were reunited a year later and I moved here to be closer to Tahnee."

"And Kristen?"

"She's the high-flyer of the Lewis trio. Has an apartment in the snazzy Arcadia Towers in Sydney, though spends most of her time jetting around the world."

"Sounds glamorous."

Carissa nodded, exceedingly proud of her corporate sister and wishing they could spend more time together. "She's gorgeous."

"Must be a family trait," he said, staring at her with those melted chocolate eyes, making her feel like she was the only woman in the world he'd ever said that too. Which couldn't be true, of course. Molly was a beautiful child and must take after her mother with her fair colouring.

"Thanks. And you've met Tahnee at the Easter pageant. She's an illustrator for children's books."

"Sounds like you're all talented too. What made you decide to open a fairy shop?"

Whether it was the intimacy of the restaurant with its muted candlelight, burgundy walls and plush velvet chairs or the genuine interest of the man sitting opposite, she found herself telling him the truth rather than the flippant answer she'd prefer.

"Ever since I was a kid, I liked make-believe stuff. It helped me cope with everyday life so after I did a marketing degree at uni I used the money my real parents left us to buy the shop. The price was much cheaper than anything similar in Sydney, with the added bonus of being close to Tahnee."

He hesitated as if reluctant to ask anything further before

continuing. "By your emphasis on real parents and alluding to having to cope with life as a kid, I take it you had a tough time with your adoptive family?"

"Understatement of the year."

The bitterness rose as always whenever she thought of Ron and Betty Lovell and she swallowed it down with effort. "But hey, let's not talk about that. They provided for me, I made it and here I am, a big girl capable of looking after herself. How about you? Tell me the Brody Elliott story."

As expected, the shutters came down, making his dark eyes unreadable. "What do you want to know?"

Could she press him about Jackie? He'd just given her the perfect opportunity to ask about his wife and in turn, bring up the topic of Molly. Taking a fortifying sip of wine, she said, "Tell me about your wife."

Pain bracketed his mouth and he hesitated, before saying, "That's easy. I killed her."

Chapter 13

Brody watched Carissa's expressive eyes widen in shock. He'd known having dinner with her might open a can of worms but he'd gone ahead and done it anyway. And now he owed her some kind of explanation, though for the life of him he'd rather talk about anything else but this.

"You know she died four years ago, right?"

Carissa nodded and leaned forward, as if prompting him to continue.

"Jackie was killed in a head-on collision by a speeding motorist."

"But that doesn't make you responsible. Cops do their best with silly drivers who speed and you can't get them all."

"That's where you're wrong. I *am* responsible. I pulled over the guy who killed her about two years earlier and know what I did? I let the bastard go. No fine, no hauling his ass in for using his car as a lethal weapon. Uh-uh. I gave him a verbal warning that amounted to a slap on the wrist to a young punk like him. And want to know why?"

She remained silent, staring at him with pity etched across

her beautiful face and damn it, he didn't want her pity. He wanted to make her understand, to make her see why all he could ever be was a friend.

He'd like to drop his guard altogether, to stop indulging in his private pity party that had been going on for the last four years and take a chance on love again. But he couldn't. His guilt had become his safety net, his protection mechanism against the pain and it was too damn soon to let go of it yet.

Just being with her like this was a step in the right direction and hopefully, if he took it slow, he could become a fully functioning guy again, one who could open his heart to a world of possibilities.

Starting with the special woman sitting opposite.

"Tell me," she said softly, her fingers fidgeting with the napkin in front of her, twisting it over and over, similar to how his gut felt right now.

"I'm responsible because the jerk reminded me of myself at his age. I was that guy ten years ago: brash, cocky, king of the world. Totally invincible, especially behind the wheel of my hotted up Ute. And I could talk my way out of any situation, just like this guy. So I let him off." He shrugged and looked away, not wanting to see the pity change to loathing in her eyes. "Basically, I signed my wife's death warrant that night. And left Molly without a mother."

"It's not your fault." She reached across the table and squeezed his hand, tugging on it. "Brody, look at me."

He finally met her gaze but rather than seeing loathing, he saw tears, and they affected him more than if she'd said she hated him. He'd made her cry? Great, so much for solidifying their friendship tonight.

"Brody, you've got a wonderful daughter who loves you, who needs you, and that's what counts. You can't change the past, no matter how much you wish you could. You—"

"But I could've done something, don't you see?" Pain

ripped through him, the type of pain that no amount of placating words could ever erase. "I took it too easy on that guy, just because I saw what I wanted to see. I let personal judgement affect my duty as a cop, something I swore I'd never do. And it cost me, big time."

"Is that why you quit your job?"

He shook his head. "I didn't quit until last year. I stayed on the force for three years after Jackie's death, wanting to make the bad guys pay more than ever. And to see that little punk get what he deserved, a hefty jail sentence."

His fellow officers had understood his thirst for vengeance though somehow, convicting the jerk hadn't helped. Nothing had.

"So he's in jail still?"

He nodded. "Not that it made me feel any better. The guy gets a few years for vehicular manslaughter, I get the life sentence."

"It doesn't have to be that way," she murmured, reaching out to cup his cheek, running her thumb over his lips in an attempt to smooth out the tense lines he knew would be puckering his mouth. He'd seen those same lines in the mirror every day for four years now and as much as he tried to smile, especially for Molly, some days it was too hard.

He stilled beneath her touch, his guilt at losing Jackie replaced by another form of guilt, the illicit pleasure he derived from Carissa's gentle touch.

She must've seen the change in his eyes, for her hand dropped and she resumed toying with the napkin. Crazily, he missed her touch.

"It's the only way I know," he said, and sadly, it was true. His guilt over Jackie's death tainted the way he looked at life, from the way he shunned other people to his over protectiveness with Molly.

"Well, it's time for a change." She leaped to her feet and he stared at her, wondering if she would run out of the restaurant now he'd told her what a sad case he was.

Instead, she grabbed his hand and pulled him to his feet and they stood there, holding hands, only one of them knowing what the hell was going on and it sure wasn't him.

"From this moment on, Brody Elliott, you will look at life with a glass-half-full attitude. No more self-pity. No more blame. Fate is a fickle thing and no one can control it, even a big, strong guy like you. And in commemoration of this momentous change, I say we do something you probably haven't done in a long time."

"What's that?"

Standing this close to her, enveloped in her signature rose scent which he loved, his imagination took flight. There were lots of things he hadn't done in a long time, most of them things he shouldn't be contemplating doing with his *friend*.

"Let's dance."

"Dance?" His feet mechanically followed her to the outdoor terrace where a groovy jazz trio were playing soulful ballads. Amazingly, he hadn't even heard the music since they started talking, his attention had been totally focussed on Carissa.

"Yeah, dance. Help you lighten up. Have fun again." She slid into his arms as if she'd been made for him, not giving him a chance to bolt into the nearby bushes before she found out he had two left feet.

Feeling self-conscious, he held her close and tried to relax, swaying in time with the music.

"You're doing good, Elliott. Real good," she murmured, resting her head against his chest and looping her arms around his neck.

She moulded perfectly to him, her breasts pressing against his chest, her hips cradled within his and as the soft saxophone drifted on the humid evening air, something unfurled within him.

And that something was hope.

Chapter 14

Carissa hated seeing anyone hurt. She'd lived a lifetime with the wasted emotion herself and she'd be damned if she sat back and let Brody stew any longer.

Little wonder the guy hid away, rarely smiled, drove like an old man, and bit everyone's head off. He'd been carrying this guilt around for years and it had eaten away at him, sapping him until he had nothing left to give. Blaming himself for his wife's death must affect everything he did—or didn't do, like give his full attention to a daughter who so obviously craved it.

Distracting him had been her number one priority minutes earlier but now that she was folded in Brody's strong arms, her soft bits pressed against his hard bits and enjoying the contact way too much, she wondered at the wisdom of it all.

Being friends was good. Friends supported each other, opened up to one another, leaned on each other in their time of need.

However, with her body plastered against his and his woody aftershave infusing her senses, she was having some decidedly *un*-friendly thoughts.

"Do you always see the good in people?" he whispered against her ear, his breath blowing gently on her skin and scattering goose bumps over her body.

"I try," she mumbled, too scared to move her head in case her face came all-too-close to his and in the event that happened, with the direction her thoughts were going, who knew what she might do. "This may sound corny and you can blame it on my job, but the world can be a magic place if you look at it the right way."

"Magic, huh?"

He pulled away from her slightly, placed a finger under her chin and tilted her head up.

Uh-oh. By the gleam in his eyes, it looked like his thoughts were heading down a similar path to hers.

"Yeah, magic," She mumbled as his head descended towards her, the first tentative touch of his lips on hers reinforcing her belief in all things enchanted.

For a man who appeared tough, his kiss was anything but, his mouth roving over hers with slow, gentle mastery.

Wow...

She'd been kissed by her string of loser boyfriends before but never like this. Brody deepened each kiss, challenging her to match him with every sweep of his tongue, with every nibble of his teeth along her bottom lip. And she did, her lips clinging to his for more, allowing the series of slow, shivery kisses to reach into her soul and soothe the need for him that burned there. The need she'd been so determined to ignore in the name of friendship.

He tasted of blackcurrant and spice, a delicious fruity combination from the wine, and she couldn't get enough.

However, like all things magical, reality had to intrude on fantasy at some point and Brody broke the kiss, his lips lingering on hers for an extra second before easing away.

"You're right. It's time I entered the real world again if

that's the type of welcome I get." His stunned gaze focussed on her mouth again, before he met her eyes. "Now, how about dessert?"

He took hold of her hand and she followed him inside, dazed, elated and thoroughly confused.

She was happy for Brody, she really was if he'd finally decided to come out of his shell. But after that kiss, what did that mean for her? For them?

Magic, schmagic, she thought, making a mental note to stop believing in the tales she told the children at her fairy parties.

———

"That was some evening." Carissa leaned against the car seat and patted her stomach, wondering if the grubs and quandongs were having a party of their own in there. She'd eaten so much she could burst but the food had been delicious, as had the company, as she cast Brody a quick glance.

"So you had a good time?"

"The best," she sighed and closed her eyes, reliving the exact moment when his lips had touched hers, the same moment she'd stopped kidding herself he was just a friend.

She liked Brody Elliott. A lot. Though she'd be a fool to dump her budding feelings on him now, when the guy was only just facing up to his past. She may live in fairyland during the day but she wasn't a complete moron.

"Not sure if I said this earlier or if I say it enough, but thanks, Carissa, especially for what you do with Molly."

Molly. In all the baring-of-the-soul stuff and that amazing kiss, she'd forgotten to talk to him about his daughter.

"Speaking of Molly, I wanted to discuss something with you."

"Shoot."

She quirked an eyebrow at him in the muted light cast by a streetlamp and said, "Is that cop humour?"

He held up his hands as if she'd bailed him up and smiled. "Hey, at least it's humour. Give me a break. I'm rusty on the funny stuff, okay?"

"Yeah, okay." A wry grin spread across her face and she hoped he'd keep humour in mind when she confronted him about Molly. "Listen, I know you're a great dad and you love Molly very much, but she's kind of hung up over her mum's death. Maybe she takes her cue from you?"

His smile vanished and telltale crinkle between his brows reappeared. "What are you trying to say?"

Taking a deep breath, she blundered on. "By your own admission, you've been moping around over Jackie's death for the last few years, beating yourself up over it. Molly notices stuff like that. She's mentioned how sad you are to me. You need to talk to her about her mum and how much she loves her and what heaven's like, that sort of thing. She's a clever little girl who craves her daddy's attention and I think you should give her more of it."

"Are you saying I'm a bad father?" If his frown deepened any more, it would split his face in two.

"No, of course not. I'm just telling you what I see."

"And what you see is my daughter needing more attention, right?"

"Right."

"Well, thanks for pointing that out, Miss childcare-worker-of-the-year. I didn't know you were such an expert, otherwise I'd have hired you to care for Molly full time."

"Don't be an idiot."

His words cut to the core but she wouldn't let him see how he'd hurt her. She was doing this for Molly, the little girl she loved, and if Brody wanted to slip back into bad-mood territory so quickly, she'd deal with it.

"Great. So not only am I a bad parent, I'm an idiot too. Thanks a lot." He turned away from her and stared out the windscreen, arms folded, rigid neck muscles, his whole body language screaming uptight.

So much for magic.

"Brody, look, I think—"

"You shouldn't spend so much time with Molly. If you think I'm so lousy as a parent, let me spend some more time with her without your constant interference."

"Is that what you really want?" she asked, her heart breaking for the predicament she'd brought on herself. Perhaps honesty wasn't the best policy in this case? And just when things were going so great. Why couldn't she keep her big mouth shut?

However, before Brody could respond, his cell rang and he fished it out of his pocket. "Hello?" He paused. "When? What happened?" His panic-stricken voice chilled her blood and she turned to him, shocked by his appearance. His tanned face had paled, leached of every ounce of colour, and sunk in on itself, ageing him ten years right in front of her eyes.

"Are you sure she's going to be alright?" He gripped the steering wheel so tight his knuckles stood out white and she had to refrain from leaning over and offering whatever comfort she could.

If something had happened to Molly...No, she wouldn't even go down that track.

"I'll be there in ten minutes," he said, disconnecting the call, sliding the cell into his pocket, and turning the ignition.

"What's happened?" She had to ask, even though deep down she already knew the answer.

"It's Molly." His voice shook and tears shimmered in his eyes, compelling her to breach the short distance between them and lay a comforting hand on his arm. "There's been an accident. I have to go."

Carissa didn't push him for details nor did she budge. He probably wanted her to get out of the car after their discussion but there was no way that was going to happen. She loved Molly and wanted to see for herself that the little darling would be all right.

"Come on then. Let's go," she said, snapping her seat belt in place and silently praying that fate hadn't been so cruel in robbing Brody of another person he loved.

Chapter 15

"Daddy!" Molly opened her arms as Brody ran into the ER cubicle, his heart in his mouth.

No matter how much Daisy had reassured him over the phone that his precious little girl was okay, he'd hardly been able to breathe on the way over, his mind conjuring up all sorts of nasty visions of Molly lying bruised and battered. Or worse. And dredging up a host of memories that left him reeling to this day.

Memories of how he'd got the call out four years ago, how he'd first came upon the mangled wreckage of the red SUV on the highway, how he'd thought the car was similar to Jackie's, and how his heart had been ripped out when he'd caught sight of his wife's lifeless head lolling on the headrest, vacant eyes staring heavenward where he hoped she rested peacefully.

Memories were the pits and he'd sworn over his wife's dead body that he would protect their daughter with every fibre of his being.

So much for promises.

He'd been out having the time of his life with another woman when he should've been keeping his promise to Jackie.

"Are you okay, munchkin?" He enveloped Molly in his arms and buried his face in her neck, inhaling the smell uniquely hers, a combination of raspberry bubble bath, strawberry shampoo and sweet little girl.

She squirmed in his arms and he released her, holding onto her hand with the intention of never letting go. "Uh-huh. But my head hurts. See? I've got sewing up there and everything."

He winced at the sight of several stitches along her forehead near the hairline and the large, purplish lump that accompanied them.

"Jessie and I were playing hide and seek and I hid under a table but when she found me, I ran out and hit my head. Jess is my bestest friend and it's not her fault so can I still play with her when I'm all better? Please, Daddy? Can I?"

Molly stared up at him with saucer-like blue eyes so like her mother's, and though he'd grown immune to Jackie's similar ploy to wheedle something out of him early in their marriage, he was a pushover when it came to their daughter.

"Sure, sweetheart. It was an accident and when you're feeling better, you can play with Jessie again."

"Yippee!" Molly clapped her hands together before tears filled her eyes and she held a hand up to her head. "Ouch. My head hurts, Daddy. Can you make the pain go away?"

Swallowing to dislodge the tennis ball sized lump of emotion lodged in his throat, he said, "You bumped your head, munchkin, that's why it hurts. If you rest and have some medicine, the pain will go away."

"Promise?"

Once again, Molly's big blue eyes beseeched him, the shimmer of tears reaching a fist into his gut and twisting until he could hardly see straight.

He nodded and smoothed a few wispy strands of hair from her cheeks. "You shut your eyes for now and it will all be better in the morning."

"Don't leave me, Daddy," she murmured, her eyes fluttering with fatigue as she battled sleep.

"I'll be right here, sweetheart." He dropped a light kiss on her cheek before tucking the sheet around her as she slipped into slumber, and he left the cubicle.

"Is she okay?" Carissa flew to his side and grabbed hold of his arm as soon as he emerged.

He nodded and rubbed a hand over his face, wondering if he'd ever grow used to the monstrous responsibility of fatherhood. He cherished every minute with Molly, though just when he thought he had a handle on the constant fear one day she'd be taken from him, this happened.

The fear was always there, a faithful companion that never left his side, and with it came the knowledge that whatever choices he made in his life, whatever he did, it all came back to the little girl laying on the bed behind the hospital curtain.

He would have to do better, that's all. And being distracted by thoughts of anything more than friendship with the beautiful woman hanging onto his arm this very minute were not helping.

Shrugging off Carissa's hand, he said, "She'll be fine. The doc said it's a mild concussion. Once she's slept it off and the stitches heal, she'll be right."

"Thank goodness." Carissa stepped back from him and he hated the hurt he glimpsed in her eyes, and the fact he'd put it there.

She'd been amazing tonight, listening to him, supporting him, making him realise there was a life for him to lead. She genuinely cared about other people, particularly kids, if her dressing down about how he'd been neglecting Molly was any indication.

Deep down, he knew she was right. He never bought Molly little surprises like the hair bows or the bracelet she'd received from Carissa and he knew he avoided talking about Jackie with his daughter.

However, he couldn't handle this now. He needed to focus on Molly and he sure as hell didn't need Carissa hanging around to remind him of how great she was or what he'd be missing out on by stomping on any possibility of a relationship between them.

For as much as he'd decided to start living again, he knew now wasn't the time. Molly's accident tonight had been a sign. He had to focus on his daughter, repair the damage he'd done by not paying her enough attention and only then could he move forward into a future for himself.

"Here." He fished the car keys from his pocket and tossed them to her. "You take my car. I'm spending the night here."

She caught the keys in a reflex reaction and stared at them like she'd never seen the bits of metal before.

"You sure everything's okay?" Her gaze sought his, seeking reassurance he couldn't give.

He couldn't give her much at all right now.

"Molly is fine, I'm fine," he snapped, feeling like a jerk when she flinched.

But maybe that was a good thing? If he pushed her away now, shattered the illusion of close camaraderie that had developed over the last few hours, the last few months if he were completely honest with himself, surely she'd take the hint they couldn't share anything more?

Theoretically, he had to do this, though in practice, with the woman he'd grown exceedingly fond of staring at him like he'd morphed into a monster, he softened his stance.

"Look, thanks for being here but I need to be alone with Molly right now. You should go home."

"Okay." She shrugged and turned away but not before he saw the glimmer of tears in her eyes.

Hell.

He was doing this for her own good. He had nothing to give her, not now, perhaps not ever. Molly was his number one priority and tonight's drama reinforced that.

Though making a woman cry wasn't his style and he hated the feeling gnawing at his gut that he'd disappointed her in some way.

"Carissa?"

"Yes?" She spun around so quickly it took every ounce of willpower not to drag her into his arms and cradle her close.

"Thank you."

He intended to plant a brief, impersonal kiss on her cheek but she turned her head at the last second and his lips landed on hers, their pliant softness enticing him to linger longer than necessary.

And for one sweet moment, he was happy to prolong the contact, to lose himself in the possibility of what may be.

Before reality crashed in, fuelled by hospital sounds that included a crying child and he pulled away, sent her a brief nod and strode back into Molly's cubicle, intent on fulfilling his parental responsibility at the expense of his heart.

Chapter 16

The next evening, Carissa glanced out her front window repeatedly, waiting for a sign of life at the Elliott household. Brody had arrived home with Molly around two this afternoon and carried her into the house, the little girl clutching a giant teddy bear that was almost as big as her, and it had taken all her willpower not to rush over to the house and see if Molly was okay.

However, she didn't want to intrude and had thrown herself into a baking frenzy, making enough choc-peppermint cookies, brownies, and lemon slice to feed half the town. Besides, Brody had made it more than clear last night he didn't need her let alone want her around and she wanted to give father and daughter some breathing space, just as he'd asked.

At six o'clock, the front door at the Elliott's opened and Molly stuck her head out, the white bandage on her forehead glowing like a beacon in the rays of the setting sun.

That was all the encouragement Carissa needed to grab the box of brownies she'd packed earlier and all but run across the lawn towards Molly.

"Carissa, look at my head. It's all banged up." Molly

proudly pointed to her forehead and Carissa tried not to grimace as she spied the size of the purple lump poking out from the bottom of the bandage.

"Yeah, I can see that. How are you feeling, sweetie?"

"Much better. Daddy bought me a teddy who has a bandage on his head too, so I can look after him and he can look after me."

"That's good."

She wanted to ask 'where's your daddy?' but bit her tongue. The way she was feeling right now, Brody was the last person she wanted to see. He'd hurt her badly, when she'd promised herself she wouldn't let any man do that to her again. Stupidly, she'd been so busy telling herself she didn't want a relationship that she'd forgotten how addictive being friends with a guy could be, especially one as sexy as her neighbour. She'd opened her heart to him as a friend, and had it broken by him when she finally acknowledged he meant so much more.

"Are those for me?" Molly's eyes grew wide as she pointed to the candy-striped box tied in red ribbon in Carissa's hands.

"Uh-huh. Brownies just for you."

"Yummy." Molly rubbed her tummy with one hand while reaching for the box with the other. "I bet brownies are real good for sore heads."

Carissa laughed and bent down to hug Molly, thankful the little girl seemed unharmed apart from the egg-sized bump on her forehead.

"Hey, Carissa."

The door swung open fully and Brody stepped out onto the porch, dark rings of fatigue circling his eyes, his hair uncombed and a five o'clock shadow bristling along his jaw. He looked like hell and all she wanted to do was wrap her arms around him and comfort him. But she couldn't. In fact, she probably wouldn't get the opportunity to get as close to him as she had last night ever again.

If he didn't want her spending time with Molly he sure wouldn't want her anywhere near him and the injustice of it all ravaged her anew.

"Hi, Brody. I just came over to drop some brownies off and to see how Molly's doing."

"Brownies are good for sore heads, aren't they, Daddy?" Molly clutched the box as if it contained priceless jewels, looking to her father with a cheeky grin on her face as if daring him to disagree.

"Sure are," he said, winking at Molly and dropping a kiss on top of her head.

"Thanks," he said, resting a hand on Molly's shoulder, the icy disdain she'd glimpsed in his eyes at the hospital last night replaced by a wary warmth.

"No problems. I'll leave you to it."

"Thanks, Carissa. Dad said I can go to school tomorrow and he's going to work."

Work? Since when did Brody have a job? And why hadn't he told her about it over dinner? Then again, perhaps he'd been too busy fielding her other personal questions, like how his wife had died and did he still love her?

He'd answered both questions, the first with words, the second with actions. It didn't take an Einstein to figure out why he'd pushed her away at the hospital. If the guy had guilt issues about being responsible for his wife's death, it would be nothing on how guilty he'd feel after kissing her.

Carissa had practically invited that kiss and any hot-blooded male would've responded. However, Brody wasn't just any male. He was a guy so in love with his dead wife's memory he hadn't been socialising in four years, had shut himself away from the world, and pushed away anyone who came too close. And with that kiss, with their developing friendship, she'd obviously got way too close.

"You've found a job?"

He nodded. "Yeah. Molly, why don't you take those brownies inside and I'll be in soon?"

"Okay, Dad. Thanks for the brownies, Carissa. Bye."

"Bye sweetie. See you soon." But sadly she wouldn't, not if Brody had his way.

"Must be some job if you can't talk about it in front of Molly."

"She looks tired. I don't want her spending too much time out here with the way she's feeling."

Uh-oh. Looked like Molly's accident had notched up Brody's over protectiveness and she hoped he wouldn't take her advice too literally. Molly needed more attention, not smothering.

"So what's the job?"

"Daisy suggested I put some of my old training to use and open up a half-way house for kids. Sort of like a career's counsellor, big brother kind of thing, a place where local kids can just hang out, play a bit of sport, have a chat if they need to. It's in the early stages but I'm pretty excited about it."

"That's great. This town has needed something like that for ages, especially for the teenagers. Most of them hang out at the skateboard ramp looking bored."

He shrugged off her admiration as if it meant little. "I've seen what boredom can do to kids. Some of them run away to Sydney and end up in all sorts of nasty situations. I worked the King's Cross beat in my rookie year and what I saw wasn't pretty, so I've had an interest ever since. Even did a social work course part time, just so I could get a handle on what these kids think, what they go through. Looks like it'll come in handy now."

While she couldn't help but admire his crusade, a small

part of her couldn't ignore the fact that he had a child of his own at home, a needy child who could do with a little more of her father's attention.

"Sounds like you'll have your hands full. Good luck with it."

"Thanks."

An awkward silence ensued and Carissa missed the easy-going camaraderie of the previous evening. As far as she could see, Brody was getting his life back on track: new town, new job, renewed enthusiasm. Pity he couldn't go the whole way and dim the torch he still held for his wife.

"Okay. Guess I'll be seeing you."

He raised his hand in a half-hearted wave. "Yeah. See you."

He couldn't look less enthused if he tried and as she trudged across the lawn towards her place, she blinked back tears.

Losing a friend would've been bad enough but since that scintillating kiss last night and the feelings it had made her acknowledge, losing Brody now hurt a whole lot more.

Chapter 17

"So how was dinner the other night?" Tahnee munched through her second croissant of the day and rolled her eyes in bliss. "I haven't seen or heard from you since. Must've been some night."

Yeah, some night. Carissa had finally got Brody to open up, only to lose him in the process. Some night.

"Dinner was lovely. You were right, the food at Kangaroo Corner is superb. I ate—"

"Sis, I'm not interested in your culinary explorations. Tell me about big, bad Brody. Anything going on between you two?"

"No. He's a friend."

Though perhaps she should say he *was* a friend. She hadn't seen him since she'd dropped the brownies off the other night and true to his word, she hadn't seen Molly either.

She missed them both more than she could possibly imagine and had no idea how to rectify the situation. So he'd taken her advice to spend more time with Molly onboard? Why did it have to be at her expense? Couldn't he see how much Molly meant to her? How much *he* meant to her?

"Then why the glum look? You two have an argument or something?"

"Or something," Carissa muttered, laying down a half-eaten croissant, her first, which showed just how awful she felt. Even the melt-in-your-mouth chocolate and banana flakiest-crescents-on-the-planet held no appeal.

"Ohhh...I get it." Tahnee brushed crumbs off her jeans, sat back and tucked her legs beneath her. "It's like that."

"Like what?"

"Sis, if I have to tell you, you're in worse shape than I thought."

"Humour me."

"Okay. The way I see it, you two have been friends for months now, you spend more time with his daughter than the great-aunt, he finally asks you out on a date, and now you look like all the fairies in your shop have come to life and run off with the rest of the merchandise. Can only mean one thing."

Tahnee didn't have to spell it out. Carissa had spent the last few nights tossing and turning, trying to evaluate her feelings, knowing the answers but deliberately avoiding asking the tough questions.

Did she love Molly enough to be her mum? Yes.

Did she want to be part of their family? Yes.

Did she love Brody? Ummm...

She faltered at that last one time and time again, not willing to go there, not willing to open herself up to the possibility of being hurt.

He didn't love her, he loved another woman, one she could never compete with. Why put herself through that?

Then this morning, as dawn had filtered through her gossamer-thin curtains, she'd had a light bulb moment.

She was doing the same thing he was: shying away from taking a risk, from living life to the full, from opening herself up to the possibility of love...and the possibility of heart ache.

And in that instant, as soft sunlight flooded her room in a golden glow, she knew the answer to that last question.

Yes. She loved Brody.

The part she hadn't quite figured out yet was what she was going to do about it.

"It can only mean one thing, huh?" Hugging her knees to her chest, Carissa rocked back and forth on the floor, staring up at her sister who sat on the couch with a grin on her face. "So what's this one thing you're gibbering on about?"

"Time to pull out the big guns."

"Which are?"

"Sun, surf and sand." Tahnee ticked the list off her fingers while Carissa wondered if she came from another planet. She had no idea what her sister was talking about half the time and now was no exception.

"Huh?"

"You two need a getaway. Somewhere away from here, where you can really unwind, talk, get rid of all this pent-up tension. Go to Bondi, have a swim, drink lattes at the cafés, let your hair down."

"Have you lost your marbles? He'd never go for that." And she'd be way too embarrassed to ask him.

Tahnee shrugged, stretched her arms and studied her French-manicured fingernails. "Fine. Have it your way. But seriously, Sis, you need to do something, otherwise I can see you two dancing around each other for years to come. Don't be boring."

What was wrong with that? Boring was good. Boring was safe.

But hadn't she realised in the wee small hours of this morning she didn't want to play it safe?

———

Feeling like a fool, Carissa peeped out the front window of the shop every few minutes, wishing Brody would hurry up and arrive before she lost the last of her already dwindling supply of courage.

She'd mulled over Tahnee's suggestion for a week, a long week in which she'd seen Molly once and even less of Brody, who vanished into his house quicker than a mouse down a hole whenever he stepped from his car. What did he think she would do, ambush him?

Like now?

Telling her conscience to shut up, she locked the cash register for the night and flipped the sign on the front door to closed. Besides, this wasn't an ambush. She just needed to see the guy, to spend more than two seconds with him to say her piece and be done with it.

If she didn't pluck up the courage to take the plunge this one time, she'd spend her whole life wondering 'what if' and she didn't want to do that. She'd wasted enough years doing that as a child, wondering 'what if her parents had lived', 'what if she'd never been separated from her sisters', 'what if the Lovells had never adopted her'? Pointless questions and she'd learned to get on and do things without dwelling on the past, without wishing she could change things.

Now if only she could instil some of that wisdom into Brody…

A sharp knock on the door brought her out of her reverie and she smiled, flipped the lock and beckoned him in.

"Sounded like it was an emergency," Brody said, glancing around the shop as if he expected to see a burst water main or the ceiling collapsed. "I came as fast as I could and I've got my tools in the car."

"Ooh, there you go again, saying the *tool* word."

He managed a tight grin and followed her into the shop. "So, what needs fixing?"

"Us."

She plunged straight in, not seeing the point in messing about. They'd wasted enough time and if she didn't get a good night's sleep soon, the bags under her eyes would soon have their own hand luggage.

"Us?" He gaped at her in open-mouthed shock and if the situation wasn't so serious, she would've laughed.

"Let me guess. According to you, there is no us."

A wary expression crept into his eyes as his gaze darted around the room as if seeking a quick escape. "We're friends, Carissa."

"Good. In that case, what do you say to a weekend in Sydney? We can chill out, take in a movie, go to the beach. Just have some fun." Her words came out in a rush and she wondered if they sounded as crazy to him as they did to her.

What had she been thinking? He wouldn't go for this, not in a million years, but at least she'd get some answers sooner than later.

He stared at her, incredulous. "Are you out of your mind?"

"Hmm...tell me how you really feel," she said, propping against the counter while wishing for a hole to open up in the star-covered carpet beneath her feet.

"Where's all this coming from?" He took a step towards her before coming to an abrupt stop, obviously having second thoughts about getting too close to the crazy woman. "We have one dinner together, share a kiss, and you want to go away together?"

She stared at him, knowing the sheer unadulterated longing in her eyes would be enough to scare him away if her words didn't. "I thought that maybe our friendship had developed into something more, that you might want to explore what that is."

For one, interminable moment, she was sure his eyes

reflected the longing in hers, before he blinked and ran a hand through his hair. "I can't."

"Can't or won't?"

Couldn't he see what she was trying to do here? She wanted to give them a chance, to see if the tiny flame between them was worth fanning into a raging inferno. It may not be forever but she had to try.

She didn't care if Brody couldn't love her as much as his wife. She loved him and that would be enough for the both of them. For now.

Sure, she wanted a future. But from where she stood, she'd settle for here and now.

"Carissa, you're a wonderful woman. And you'll make some guy very lucky one day." He glanced away as he said the words, focussing on the front door as if he wanted to bolt.

"But not you, right?"

He shook his head, his sombre expression reminiscent of the first time she'd seen him, glowering at her over their fence. "I can't give you what you want."

You can, she wanted to scream.

She wanted to lay out all the simple, logical reasons why they belonged together, to try and convince him, to make him see sense.

Instead, she blinked back the tears that threatened to pour down her face and hit him where he was most vulnerable. "What about Molly? What about what she wants? Can't you see she needs a mother?"

His face contorted into a grief-stricken mask and she stepped back, fearing she'd gone too far.

"Molly had a mother and you know what? I took that away from her. Never again."

"But that's crazy, I won't leave you. I love—" she stopped herself in time. No use revealing her feelings when he was intent on throwing everything she had to offer back in her face. If he couldn't see the logic in any of her arguments, what hope did she have?

"—Molly," she finished lamely. "I'd never do anything to hurt her."

He waved away her words as if they meant nothing. "Not intentionally, maybe. But life happens, Carissa. I won't have my little girl grow to depend on you, only to have circumstances intervene and rip her heart out all over again."

She wanted to rant at the injustice of it all. She wanted to swear and stamp her feet, to let him know exactly what she thought of his insane logic. Instead, she settled for words.

"Brody, I care about you. We make a good team, surely you can see that?"

His lips compressed in a thin, rigid line and she knew the stubbornness of a whole pack of donkeys would have nothing on this guy.

"It's not enough."

"What do you want from me?"

She hoped he'd say *you* but she wasn't delusional. If he loved her, he might be willing to take a chance but as things stood, he was so wrapped up in his love for his dead wife he couldn't see what was right in front of him: a woman who loved him.

Before she could move, he stepped forward and cupped her cheek, his thumb brushing along her jaw line, the tenderness in his eyes undoing her completely. "I want you to be happy."

"I want that too," she whispered, turning her face slightly to bring her lips in contact with his thumb.

He pulled away as if burned and she dashed a hand across her eyes, thankful she'd worn waterproof mascara.

"If being friends is too hard for you, maybe we shouldn't see each other anymore?" Once again, he looked over her shoulder, unable to meet her eyes and she liked to think the thought of not seeing her brought on the flash of pain that contorted his face.

"What about my relationship with Molly?"

"I don't know. Maybe you're too attached to her? Maybe it's best if she doesn't see you?"

"Best for who? Not Molly, that's for sure. She's grown attached to me whether you like it or not and the feeling is entirely mutual."

Damn him. Why couldn't he see she was the best thing for both of them?

"I'll be the judge of what's best for my daughter." He turned and headed for the door without a backward glance.

Making a last ditch stand, she opted for brutal honesty, hoping it would get through to him. "You're being selfish. Just because of your feelings for Jackie, you're not willing to take a chance again. You're suffering because of it and so is your daughter. You're self-centredness is—"

"That's enough." His harsh words whipped out and lashed her with pain anew.

"So that's it?" She half sobbed, knowing there was nothing worse than a clingy female but unable to stop the deep-seated desire to hang onto the man she loved.

For one, glorious moment he turned back, his expression faltered, and she thought she saw more than pain there, a glimmer of emotion that matched her own. However, it was gone as quickly as it had come and she knew it must've been a figment of her imagination.

Brody didn't love her. He loved his daughter, a fact she'd initially questioned. How ironic, that she now believed him—at the expense of her heart.

And she couldn't fault him for it. The man loved Molly, put her needs first, one of the many reasons she loved him for.

"You're special, Carissa." He crossed the room in three long strides, pulled her close and she leaned against him, revelling in the contact, the comforting warmth that would be ripped from her all-too-soon. "I hope you find the magic you so richly deserve."

And with that, he stepped out of their embrace and was gone.

One minute, she had the world at her feet. The next, it had tipped on its axis and spun so out of control she seriously doubted it would ever right itself again.

Chapter 18

"You're running away." Tahnee lay on Carissa's bed, chin in hands, as she watched her pack.

"I'm taking your advice and having a break," Carissa said, zipping her suitcase shut and glancing around her room for any last minute items she might need over the next few weeks. "It's been ages since I've spent time in Sydney and so what if Brody doesn't want to come? I'll have fun on my own. And no, I'm not running away."

"This, from the woman who faces battles head on? From the woman who survived living with the Lovells? From the woman who would sooner take a bullet for one of her crazy sisters than let them be hurt?"

"Who said I'd take a bullet for you?"

Tahnee leaped off the bed and enveloped her in a bear hug. "Well, maybe you didn't say that but you would, wouldn't you?"

"You're impossible." Carissa hugged her sister, amazed at how close they'd become. If only Kristen could join them in Stockton more often, their family circle would be complete. But then, she wouldn't have a vacant swank apartment in

Sydney to chill out in if her sister wasn't traipsing the world as a high-tech TV producer.

"And you love me for it." Tahnee plopped down on the bed after Carissa released her, and hugged her knees to her chest. "So the guy didn't go for the weekend away thing? Give him some time. He might still come around."

"When hell freezes over."

Brody had made his feelings perfectly clear and now Carissa had time to mull over his rejection, she couldn't blame him. The guy didn't have feelings for her. What was she going to do, manufacture them out of thin air? Sure, she believed in all things magical but this time, she was plain out of conjuring miracles.

Besides, he'd proved to her that he was a great father, that he put Molly's needs first. Pity her heart had to break in the process for her to realise it.

"Have you said goodbye to Molly yet?"

"She's coming over in ten minutes."

And Carissa was not looking forward to telling her favourite little girl that she was leaving on an indefinite holiday. She loved Molly and would miss her terribly but this was something she had to do.

Being away from the Elliotts would give her perspective on where her life was heading. Until recently, she thought she had her life all figured out. No men, no relationships, no hassles. And then she had to go and fall in love. Major pain in the ass.

"Well, don't worry about the shop. I'll hold the fort while you're away. I can draw my illustrations while manning the register."

Carissa's hand flew to her mouth. "I completely forgot. Did your publisher extend your contract?"

"You bet your sweet butt she did." Tahnee squared her shoulders and grinned. "You're looking at Australia's number one children's books illustrator. Cool, huh?"

"I'm so proud of you, Sis." Carissa plopped on the bed next to Tahnee and hugged her again. "You should've told me."

Tahnee pushed her away, laughing. "It's no biggie. Besides, your love-life dramas are much more intriguing than my itty-bitty drawings."

"Says who?" Carissa managed a wry chuckle, which died in an instant when she heard a faint knocking on the front door.

"Guess that's my cue to leave," Tahnee said, unfolding her long, denim-clad legs from the bed and shrugging into her trademark matching jacket. "Take care, Sis. And ring me if you need anything."

"You too." Carissa blinked back tears and aimed another hug her sister's way.

"Hey, enough of the mushy stuff already," Tahnee said, dropping a quick peck on her cheek and heading out the door. "I'll let the cherub in on my way out. Ciao."

Taking a deep breath, Carissa picked up the gift-wrapped box from her dressing table and clutched it to her chest, hoping Molly liked it. She wanted to give the little girl something special before she left, something that would bring her as much happiness as Molly had to her.

"Carissa. Where are you?" Molly's skipping footsteps echoed in the hallway and Carissa opened the bedroom door, clueless as to how to approach this goodbye.

Should she tell Molly the truth or sugar-coat her impending absence? What would Brody want her to do?

And then, as she crouched down, laying the box next to her on the floor and Molly flew into her arms, she thought, "*Screw Brody.*" At least he'd been right about one thing. Molly came first and she'd make damn sure the little girl knew it too.

Molly broke their hug. If it had been up to Carissa, she would've cradled her forever and never let go.

"What's in the pink box?" Molly pointed to the box on the floor, curiosity lighting her eyes. "I love pink. It's my favourite colour."

"I know."

Carissa knew everything there was to know about Molly's preferences, like her penchant for pasta, choc-chip cookies, strawberry milkshakes, and anything to do with dolls. Despite not having a mother, Molly was a healthy, well-adjusted little girl and Carissa felt bad for being overly critical of Brody and his parenting skills. The guy had done a marvellous job with Molly and a small part of her wished she'd had a chance to tell him. However, it was not to be and right now, she had to get through this farewell without bawling.

"And the purple ribbon has fairies on it." Molly's eyes grew wide with wonder and it took every ounce of Carissa's courage not to smother the little girl in another hug. "Fairies are my favourite too."

Swallowing the lump of emotion in her throat, Carissa said, "The box is for you, sweetie. It's a present."

"But it's not my birthday." A tiny frown creased Molly's forehead as her gaze stayed riveted to the box. "Or Christmas. Why did you get me a present?"

Carissa sat cross-legged on the floor next to Molly and patted the space beside her, hoping she wouldn't botch this. She had to choose her words carefully if she didn't want to upset Molly.

"It's a special present just for you." She handed the box carefully to Molly and nodded her encouragement to open it when Molly looked up at her expectantly. "I'm going on a holiday so I won't be able to play with you for a while." A *long* while if Brody had anything to do with it. "This way, you can look at your present every day and think of how much I love you."

"Wow." Molly ripped the ribbon and paper off in record

time, opened the box, and cradled the glass globe in both hands, so entranced that Carissa wondered if Molly had heard a word she'd said.

Tilting the globe upside down, Molly smiled as multi-coloured sparkles rained down on the two fairies holding hands while sitting on matching toadstools. "Look, there's one big fairy and one little one, like you and me."

Carissa nodded, not trusting herself to speak as her throat closed over with emotion again.

"Do the fairies love each other like we do?" Molly asked, peering into the globe intently as if the answer to her question lay there.

"They sure do," Carissa said, her voice tight with emotion, finding saying goodbye to Molly ten times harder than expected.

"I'll miss you." Molly shook the globe, her bottom lip wobbling as twin tears trickled down her cheeks and Carissa's heart clenched.

"Don't cry, sweetie." She pulled the little girl onto her lap and hugged her tight, raining light kisses on her face and neck until Molly giggled. "Whenever you miss me, all you have to do is look at these fairies, close your eyes, and think of how much I love you. That way, I'll never be far away."

Molly's giggles stopped abruptly and she nodded, her blue eyes solemn. "That's how Daddy says I can talk to Mummy too, with my eyes closed. She's an angel now, you know."

"I know."

Boy, did she know. Both figuratively and literally, Brody loved his dead wife so much that he couldn't see past it and wouldn't give anyone else a chance of sharing his love.

"Would you like me to put the globe back in the box? That way, you can carry it home carefully."

"Yes, please. Wait until I show Aunt Daisy." Molly slid off her lap into a crumpled heap on the floor before jumping up and dusting herself off, as resilient kids do. "She likes fairies too, you know."

Carissa smiled, repackaged the globe, and took hold of Molly's hand, leading her to the front door where she bent down and eye-balled her. "I love you, Molly."

"And I love you," Molly said, throwing her chubby arms around Carissa's neck. "I hope you come back real soon."

Carissa didn't answer. What could she say? She didn't want to lie to Molly and she had no idea when she'd be back. Who knew, maybe she'd find the perfect spot in Sydney to open a new, improved version of *Fey For Fun* and that would be that.

Good bye Stockton.

Good bye heartache.

Tahnee would understand. They'd spent the last six years living in this town, getting to know each other all over again after being separated as kids. Besides, Sydney wasn't that far away and they could visit regularly. An added bonus would be spending more time with Kristen too, if she ever stayed in one city long enough.

"Here, sweetie. Be careful." Carissa handed the box to Molly, dropped a final kiss on her forehead and tugged on her ponytail, blinking through tears as she watched Molly walk sedately across the front lawn to her house.

She'd done it. She'd said goodbye to Molly without breaking down completely.

And then it happened. Molly paused on her front doorstep, turned, and blew a kiss, the tears on her soft cheeks glinting in the fading sunlight.

"Oh, my darling girl." Carissa sobbed, returning the gesture before fleeing into the house where she could bawl in peace.

Chapter 19

"Thanks for looking after Molly, Daisy."

Brody dropped his back-pack on the kitchen bench, amazed at the exhaustion that made his muscles and joints ache as if he were eighty. Keeping up with the kids at the half way house was turning into more than a full-time job and he never seemed to have enough hours in the day to implement all the strategies he had planned.

"No need to thank me. She's been a little angel since Carissa left. Totally subdued, though I hope that's not because she's pining already."

Carissa left.

The two words penetrated his fatigue, though he must've misunderstood. Daisy probably meant she'd gone to the shop for stocktake or to work late. Or worse, perhaps she had a date?

His hands clenched into fists at the thought. He shouldn't care but he did, damn it. He cared more than he'd let her believe.

"Where did she go?" He aimed for nonchalance, filling a

glass with water from the tap and taking a sip, all the while trying to read Daisy's face.

"Sydney. She's leaving town for an indefinite period, staying at her sister's place in the city."

"*What?*" Water spluttered from his mouth in an embarrassing spray, shooting his nonchalant act down in flames.

"Didn't you know?" Daisy's smug grin didn't help matters.

"No."

How would he know, when he'd barely spoken to her since he'd turned down her invitation to go away? It had been so tempting, the thought of the two of them spending time in Sydney, just hanging out. But he wasn't a complete fool. He'd seen the sexy gleam in her blue eyes, the promise that a weekend away with her meant more. So much more.

And what had he done? Killed the gleam with a few harsh home truths, pushing her away when every cell of his body had screamed he was making a huge mistake.

Now, she'd gone and he should be glad. He should be downright ecstatic that the temptation to lose his head had been removed.

Instead, a dull ache started in the vicinity of his heart and slowly spread outward, until every bone in his weary body felt like it had been battered with a cricket bat.

Shrugging into her coat, Daisy said, "Molly got to say goodbye. Carissa gave her a special gift to remember her by, which is rather sweet, don't you think?"

He nodded mechanically, having a tough time absorbing anything Daisy was saying.

Gone. Carissa was gone.

And the pain of loss ravaged him once again.

"Daddy, you're home." Molly appeared in the doorway, dragging her feet as she shuffled into the kitchen, the complete antithesis of her usual greeting when he returned home from work and she ran through the house to leap into his arms.

"Hey, munchkin." He fixed a smile on his face, hoping it wouldn't crack with the effort. He'd never felt like smiling less, a strange phenomenon in itself, considering he hadn't smiled much in years anyway.

However, living in Stockton had changed him. He'd been happier these last few months, grinning like a clown most days, even laughing on occasion. This town had been good for him, had changed him for the better.

Or maybe he should be looking closer to home, like next door, for the person responsible for wreaking the changes with him?

"I'm sad, Daddy."

He sat on a kitchen chair and Molly clambered onto his lap, and he wrapped his arms around her waist. However, she didn't snuggle into him like she usually did. Instead, she fixed him with a sad stare. "Carissa has gone away and I miss her."

Brody stared at Daisy over his daughter's head, feeling totally helpless. Rather than lending a hand, Daisy folded her arms and quirked an eyebrow as if to say "let's see you get yourself out of this one, mister."

"Do you miss her, Daddy?"

Hell. The situation was getting more out of control by the minute. And this time, Daisy had the audacity to grin.

"Sure, sweetheart."

He *did* miss her. He'd missed her the last few days; missed seeing her cheeky smile as she teased him about something, missed the speculative stares she sent his way when she thought he wasn't looking, missed having another adult around to share the load with, to chat to while playing with Molly.

Yet he had no right to miss her. Every reason he had for

missing her amounted to seeing her as a life partner, as part of their family, and he wouldn't go there. He couldn't.

If losing Jackie had ripped him apart and he hadn't been in love with her, imagine what losing Carissa would mean if he ever lost her.

Brody sat bolt upright and tightened his grip on Molly to prevent her slipping off his lap.

But that would mean he loved Carissa...

Ah hell.

"Daddy, are you okay? You look kind of sick, like how I looked that time I ate too many choc-chip cookies."

He was sick all right. Love sick. And it taken the woman he loved to leave to give him a wake-up call.

"Daddy?"

He focussed his attention on Molly, feeling like a dazed sleepwalker stumbling through a hazy dream into consciousness. "I'm just tired, munchkin. Why don't you get ready for bed and I'll come in and read you any story you like?"

"You mean it? Even The Fairy Princess?"

His gut turned over at Molly's innocent reference, memories of a real-life fairy princess fresh in his mind. Unfortunately, he sure as hell wasn't a Prince Charming. He needed time to think, time to sort through his feelings now that he recognised them for what they were worth.

He loved Carissa. He *loved* her.

And it scared him to death.

Dropping a kiss on Molly's forehead, he said, "Yeah, even that story. Say goodnight to Aunt Daisy and I'll be in shortly."

"Thanks, Daddy. I don't feel so sad anymore. And when you come to my room, I'll show you the present Carissa got me. And it isn't even my birthday or anything." Molly waved. "Goodnight, Aunt Daisy. You'll have to come over more often now and play because I won't have Carissa to be my buddy."

He watched Molly scamper from the room and sat back, shaking his head.

"I'll be off then," Daisy said, her mouth opening as if she wanted to say something else before snapping shut again.

He couldn't blame her if she did. Daisy had been right all along. He hadn't realised what he had in Carissa until she was gone.

"Goodnight, Daisy." He stood and crossed the kitchen, opening the door for her. "And thanks again."

After closing the door he leaned against it and shut his eyes for a moment, the realisation that he loved Carissa making his head spin.

Now all he had to do was find her, do some serious grovelling and hope she had it in her generous heart to forgive him.

And love him.

Chapter 20

Carissa slipped her feet into elf slippers, padded into the kitchen, poured a glass of fruity chardonnay and slid onto one of the stainless steel barstools, taking in the impressive view of Sydney's skyline from the kitchen window. The Harbour Bridge glittered like a giant coat hanger while city lights sparkled like fairy dust on a magician's cloak.

Though she missed Stockton, relaxing in Kristen's fancy apartment was worth it for the view alone. It had been two days since she'd left town, forty-eight long hours where each moment seemed to drag into the next. She obviously needed to take time out more often if this is how she reacted to being away from the shop.

It had been too long since she'd had a proper holiday and maybe this break would give her time to plan one. And perhaps that would take her mind off Stockton and what—or should she say who—she'd left behind.

She'd thought that by leaving her problems behind she could forget about them, just like she had with the Lovells. However, she hadn't loved them how she loved Brody and Molly and leaving town only served to drive home how much she missed them, how much she wanted to be a part of their lives.

After setting her wine down she wandered into the living room, with its sleek lines and glossy chrome and leather furniture. Everything matched perfectly, from the coffee table to the coat stand and was the complete antithesis of her small, crammed cottage.

However, one similarity struck her: no family photos.

Like her, Kristen had the upbringing from hell and obviously didn't want any reminders. The only reference to family was in the luxurious master bedroom, where several large photos of the three sisters took pride of place on her dressing table and bedside tables.

Of the three of them, Kristen seemed the most aloof, the one driven to succeed professionally, as if filling a void in her life. Carissa had bonded with Tahnee much quicker, though she hoped that on Kristen's return the three of them could spend some time together, whether she decided to stay in Sydney permanently or not.

Kristen's adoptive parents had died around the same time as Betty Lovell, a year after Ron had curled up his toes, and though Carissa had escaped their dreadful home years earlier she'd attended Betty's funeral out of respect and to bury her residual animosity. Pity she couldn't have done the same with her memories.

Though all that was in the past. Her sisters were her family now. And one day, she'd have a family of her own. A family who loved her as much as she loved them.

All she had to do was stop casting the Elliotts in that role first.

As she skimmed through the magazine rack, the doorbell rang. Glancing down at her denim cut-offs, her pink silk camisole, and elf slippers, she hoped that whoever it was had the wrong apartment. In fact, they had to have the wrong place because no one knew she was here apart from Tahnee, who was minding the shop, and Kristen, who'd returned to Singapore for work.

Grinning at the image she would present to her mistaken visitor, she opened the door.

"Hey, Carissa."

Carissa's smile waned, her mouth went dry, and her heart slammed against her ribcage as her mind registered the visitor was Brody Elliott, the same Brody Elliott she'd run from, the same Brody Elliott who held her heart in the palm of his hand and squashed it regardless.

He looked incredible, living up to his bad boy persona in black jeans, a black T-shirt that looked poured on, and another haircut. Though she liked his scruffy, hair-curling-around-the-collar look, this new, sharper Brody looked like a model, the short-back-and-sides accentuating his cheekbones and adding a depth to his eyes she'd never imagined possible.

He looked heartbreakingly sexy…and she should know. He'd broken her heart without trying.

"How did you find me?" She finally managed when her tongue unglued its way from the roof of her mouth. "What are you doing here?"

"I remembered you said your sister lived in Arcadia Towers and the name Lewis was on the mailbox. As for why I'm here, I came to see you."

She kind of got that part. The part she didn't understand was why.

Sighing, she stepped away from the door. "Guess you better come in then."

"Thanks."

She willed herself not to inhale as he walked in, knowing it would resurrect a host of memories she'd rather forget. However, she had to breathe at some point and unfortunately, that time came as he brushed past her, exuding a powerful combination of the faint musk soap he used along with pheromones that were pure Brody.

She shut her eyes for a moment, desperately trying to block out the other instances she'd got close enough to smell the heady blend, like their first kiss on the dance floor and their brief farewell embrace when he'd broken her heart.

So much for forgetting. How was a woman supposed to eradicate this guy from her memory when he turned up on her doorstep smelling this good?

"I'm sorry about dropping by unannounced but I had to see you."

Her eyes flew open to find him staring at her with that intent, chocolate stare he did so well, the kind of stare that penetrated all the way down to her soul and left her strangely breathless.

"Is it Molly?"

Her heart almost stopped at the thought. How selfish could she be? Here she was, having palpitations over how sexy the guy looked and thinking how cool is was that he'd come to see her when the little girl she loved could be ill. "Is she okay? Did something happen?"

"She's fine." He grimaced. "Well, mostly."

She knew something was wrong for him to turn up here like this. Why did it have to be Molly? The little darling had been through so much all ready.

"What does that mean?"

"She misses you." He lifted a hand to run it through his hair and then stopped, as if startled to find the hair not there.

"Oh."

"I miss you," he murmured, crossing the room to stare out the window and she wondered if she'd heard correctly.

However, before she could formulate the words to ask him, he spun around and stared at her like a wild man. "Why did you bolt like that?"

"I needed some space, some time to think."

Some time to heal, and some time to stop loving him.

"You didn't even say good-bye," he muttered, sounding more like the Brody of old, grumpy and recalcitrant, despite the new look.

"Would that have changed anything?" she asked softly, still at a loss as to why he was here.

So he missed her? Big deal. That wasn't enough. She wanted love, the whole kit and caboodle. And if her brief time away had taught her anything, she wouldn't settle for anything less.

She'd been raised in a family without love, lived with two parents who tolerated each other, who may have cared about each other but rarely showed it.

Never again. She wanted more. She *deserved* more.

"Ah, hell," he said, striding across the room to stand two feet in front of her. "We want you to come back."

He looked ready to haul her into his arms but thought better of it when she took a step back.

"Why?"

"Because we miss you. I know I'm moody and grumpy and downright obnoxious at times, but for Molly's sake, will you do it?"

No mention of love. No mention of the words she so desperately needed to hear. But she gave him one last shot at it anyway.

"What are we talking about here? Are you asking me to come back to Stockton as your neighbour or something more?"

A faint colour stained his cheeks. "Why don't you come back and we take it from there?"

And just like that, *major reality check* flashed across her brain like a huge, neon sign.

Nothing had changed.

He saw her as a nice woman who loved his daughter, a woman who was good for the occasional flirtation with but nothing more. Sure, she could go back and return to being nice Carissa, caring Carissa, subservient Carissa, like she had her whole life.

She'd always settled for second best, not wanting to rock the boat. Rocking the boat caused tsunamis that could wipe out everything and wreak devastation and she had no intention of being a victim this time around. At least living with the Lovells had taught her that much.

So she had a news flash for him. Caring Carissa was taking a holiday and she had no idea when she'd be back.

"I think you should leave," she said, turning her back on him to walk into the kitchen and take a healthy swig of wine. If ever she needed false courage to deal with a situation, this was it.

"What do you expect me to say?" He followed her into the kitchen, his voice taking on a pleading tone that startled her as much as his presence here.

Shaking her head, she skirted around the island bench and headed back towards the front door, finding the confines of the kitchen claustrophobic with him in there.

"When you figure it out, let me know." She opened the door and held it for him, pointing the way out.

Shaking his head, he made to brush past her, stopping dead at the last moment and dragging her into his arms. "You want me to say I love you? Well, I do. I love you, Carissa. You'll be a great mum for Molly."

For one, heart-stopping moment, she almost capitulated. Being this close to him, touching him, hearing those three little magical words weakened her resolve.

However, she knew there was no emotion behind his profession of love. He'd blurted it out like a desperate man using whatever means necessary to get what he wanted and in this case, he wanted his daughter's friend to come home and play.

If he'd said he loved her without the tag of being a mother for Molly, she might've believed him but as it were, she was done believing in false declarations of love.

Ron Lovell had said he loved her...before locking her in a cupboard because she didn't hug him hard enough.

Betty Lovell had said she loved her...before turning a blind eye to her husband's cruelty.

And Carissa had had it up to her eyeballs with guys who'd say the L word to get something they wanted. For the losers she'd dated, it had usually been sex. With Brody, he was asking so much more and she couldn't go there, not unless she had the whole package: his commitment, his adoration, and a guarantee she was the love of his life.

Pushing him away, she stepped out of his embrace. "Good bye, Brody. Close the door on your way out."

Before she fell apart, she held her head high and walked into the bedroom, listening for the slam of the door that would signal the end of her hopes and dreams.

Though she expected it, when the sound came it didn't make it any easier and she curled up in the foetal position on her sister's king-size bed and sobbed her heart out.

Chapter 21

Brody stomped into his hotel room, grabbed a mineral water from the fridge, twisted the top off and drank deeply, wondering how he'd managed to make such a mess of things.

He'd had it all planned out. See Carissa, convince her to come home, take a chance on a relationship, give her some time to get used to the idea he loved her. Instead, she'd all but dragged his declaration out of him and rather than being romantic and special, it had sounded pathetic. Worse, he could tell she didn't believe him.

If only she loved him. He knew she cared, she'd said as much, otherwise she wouldn't have put up with his moodiness for months and she wouldn't have invited him away for a weekend. How ironic, that here they both were in Sydney as she'd wanted, but totally alone. Carissa loved Molly and he'd counted on that being enough to convince her to come home. The rest, like the three of them becoming a family, could've come later.

But something had gone horribly wrong. Whether it had been in the planning or the delivery, she'd sent him packing and he now had to resort to bringing in the big guns.

For there was no way in hell he would let her go this easily. He loved her and the next time she heard those words, he wanted her to believe them.

So plan A had been scuttled.

Time to move onto plan B...

Whatever the hell that was.

———

Carissa stepped out into the bright morning sunshine and slid her sunglasses into place, more to hide her swollen eyes than reflect the glare. She'd had a terrible night, tossing and turning; when she eventually stopped crying, that is. She hadn't cried that much since copping her first beating with a wooden spoon from Ron when she'd run away all those years ago and funnily enough, the feeling now was just the same: disillusionment, disappointment and pain.

So much pain.

Shaking her head to dispel the fog of gloom surrounding her—she'd promised herself to cheer up this morning—she fished around in her handbag for her cell. She needed to call Tahnee and check how the shop was—and to ask if her sister minded staying on for longer than anticipated.

Thanks to Brody, she'd come to a decision last night. It was definitely time for a holiday, a long, leisurely holiday in some exotic hotspot where she could unwind, have daily massages, big cocktails with little umbrellas, and not set eyes on a guy for the duration.

As her hand wrapped around her cell, something grabbed her attention and she rubbed her free hand across her eyes, wondering if the sleepless night had taken more of a toll than she thought.

Blinking, she opened her eyes and refocused. No, it wasn't a mirage.

There, on the opposite street corner, stood a billboard. Not just any billboard, but a huge billboard that up until today had advertised the latest whiz-bang sports car.

However, the car was gone, and in its place stood a bunch of giant letters, spelling out a message that had her leaning against the nearest wall for support.

I LOVE YOU, CARISSA LEWIS.

FOR YOUR BEAUTY INSIDE AND OUT, YOUR CARING, YOUR ABILITY TO BRING OUT THE BEST IN ME AND EVERYONE AROUND YOU.

YOU ARE THE ONE AND ONLY LOVE OF MY LIFE.

WILL YOU MARRY ME?

She rubbed a hand across her eyes again, opened them and took another look. Yep, the message still read the same.

"So, what do you think? Will you?"

While she'd been in a daze, Brody had sidled up to her and now stood leaning against the same wall she did as if he didn't have a care in the world.

"Are you insane?"

"Yeah. Crazy in love with you."

"But...but..."

"And your cute butt. And your smile. And your expressive eyes. And your—"

"Okay, okay. I get the picture." A tiny sliver of happiness pierced the mire of self-doubt and pain. "How? When? Why?"

"How? By calling in a few favours from the guys on the force and fire team. When? In the wee hours of this morning. Why?" He slid an arm around her waist and hugged her close. "Because I love you and want to spend the rest of my life with you."

The feel of his arm anchoring her to his side, the tenderness in his eyes, and the words she'd dreamt of hearing blurred into one, amazing kaleidoscope of joy. However, when something was too good to be true, it usually was, and at the risk of bursting the happiness bubble surrounding them, she had to ask the tough questions, silently praying he had the right answers.

"What about Jackie?"

"Huh?"

"I thought she's the love of your life and I don't want to compete with that. I *can't* compete with a dead woman."

Cradling her close, he tipped her chin up with a finger and stared into her eyes. "Jackie and I were a heat-of-the-moment item and the main reason we married is because she fell pregnant."

"Oh."

"Not long into the marriage, I realised it was a mistake, but for the sake of Molly, I stuck it out. To compound our problems, she was a lousy mother and I couldn't forgive her for that."

"So when she died, you were estranged?"

Pain flickered in his eyes and she reached out and smoothed his brow, knowing it was a futile gesture but wanting to touch him, to convey in some small way that she understood, that she sympathised.

"Emotionally, I guess we'd been estranged for a long time. And then when I realised the part I'd played in her death, I felt worse than ever."

"But it wasn't your fault. Surely you can see that?"

"Lately, I've been doing a lot of thinking and I guess it's time to stop feeling so damn guilty and get on with my life. In a way, I think I've been hanging onto the guilt to stop me from really examining how I felt at the time, and as much as I hate to admit it, relief mingled alongside the grief."

He glanced away for a moment, his gaze focussed on the

billboard before returning to look into her eyes, a new resolve adding a sheen to the dark brown depths. "It sounds like I'm sort of monster when I say it like that but in accepting my feelings as legitimate at the time, I've been able to sort through how I feel now. I was too afraid to open up to you, too afraid that if I got too close and I lost you, I wouldn't be able to cope. I didn't love Jackie and losing her ripped me apart. Loving and losing you would finish me."

Carissa had asked for answers and she'd well and truly got them. Brody Elliott was a man in touch with his feelings. He was a man who could face his demons and come through the other side with a whole new perspective on life. In short, he was a man she admired, respected and loved. And she'd make sure he knew it every day of however long they had together in this lifetime.

"That's a pretty big statement you've made up there on that billboard, Elliott."

His lopsided smile made her heart flip. "I had to do it. I didn't think you believed me last night when I said I love you. And I do, Carissa. I love you with every bone in this grumpy body. And then some."

She reached up to cradle his face in her hands, enjoying the rasp of stubble against her palms, knowing it would feel heavenly on the rest of her body.

"I love you. Grumpy bones and all. There's nothing sexier than a man in touch with his feelings and boy, have you run the gamut with those. Am I dreaming? Is this real?"

He smiled and she caressed his lips with her thumbs. "It's real, fairy princess. Believe me, with the amount of ribbing I copped from the guys over that," he pointed at the billboard, "it's real."

"If I'm a fairy princess, doesn't that make you Prince Charming?"

"Hey, let's get one thing straight. I may love you but I'm

no prince. I'll still be moody on occasion, though for the bulk of the time, I'll do my damnedest to live up to the charming part."

"In that case, how about you start by giving your princess a kiss?"

"Your wish is my command," he murmured, his lips descending to hers, unleashing the latent heat that had been bubbling between them for months.

"Jeez, why don't you get a room?" A teenager yelled as he skateboarded past at a million miles an hour and they sprung apart, laughing.

"So, your answer is yes?"

She snapped her fingers. "Did I forget about the proposal part?"

He tried a mock frown and failed. "Yeah, you did."

"Of course I'll marry you, though there is one thing we haven't discussed. How will Molly feel about all this? I don't want to do anything to hurt or frighten her."

Her heart hoped the little girl would be ecstatic at the news but the logic side of her brain, the one that remembered how she felt when finding herself lumbered with new parents, told her something quite different.

Though initially happy to leave the orphanage behind, she'd soon resented the Lovells and it looked like the feeling had been mutual. She loved Molly too much to inflict that sort of baggage on a child at her age.

Brody cupped her face and stared at her with those incredible melted-chocolate eyes. "Molly has been a major part of my decision. I think you of all people understand that. I've always put her needs ahead of my own despite what you thought at the start and this time, it just so happens our needs match. We both need you, Carissa. We both love you and can't wait for you to become a part of our family."

She swatted his hands away, tears clogging her throat.

"Where does it say in the fairy tale that the princess turns on the waterworks?"

Smiling, he dropped a light kiss on her lips and took hold of her hand. "From this moment on, we're living our own fairytale. With the happiest ever after of all."

Epilogue

"Higher, Mummy. Higher."

Carissa smiled at Brody over the skipping rope, doing as Molly asked with one hand while resting the other on her growing bump.

"Just a little while longer, munckin. Mummy's getting tired."

Molly stopped jumping immediately and rushed over to Carissa. "Is it the baby? Is he making you tired?"

Carissa squatted down with the grace of an overweight hippopotamus and pulled Molly close. "So you think it's a he, huh?"

Molly placed one hand on Carissa's swollen belly, screwed up her eyes tight as if deep in thought, and nodded. "Yep. It's a he. Has to be. Boys are always trouble."

Chuckling, Brody bent down and joined them on the lawn. "Even me?"

Doubt flickered across Molly's face as she looked into her father's face, blue eyes staring into brown. "Only sometimes."

Brody hid his face behind his hands, feigning hurt, before

splitting his fingers apart and peering out from between them. "Like when?"

"Like the time you went away to Sydney to see Carissa and didn't take me." Molly waggled a finger at Brody, and Carissa stifled a laugh. "You were in big trouble then."

Brody lowered his hands and kissed Molly on the cheek. "You're right, munchkin. But look what I brought you. Isn't Carissa a great present?"

Molly giggled and slipped a hand into hers and Brody's, completing their family circle. A circle that would soon include a precious baby as the perfect addition to the Elliott family.

Her family. Something Carissa had craved her entire life and she was so happy she could scarcely believe it.

Life didn't get any better than this. A husband who adored her, a daughter who grew even more sweet with every passing day, and a new life to seal the bond they'd created. Together.

"You're right, daddy. You brought me a mummy and that's the best present ever!"

"Hear, hear," Brody said, sending Carissa a look of such love, such tenderness, that she knew she'd come home.

If you enjoyed this romance, please consider leaving a review to help new readers discover Nicola's books.

Want to read Tahnee and Kristen's stories?

THE SHY GUY

Reclusive children's author Bo Bradford is on a tight deadline and the last thing he needs is a new illustrator barging into his orderly world and turning it upside down. Being the number one bestselling author means everything to him and no way will he let some bubbly, sassy illustrator disrupt it, no matter how badly he wants her.

Tahnee Lewis falls for Wally the Wombat like the rest of Australia, but when she lands the dream job of illustrating Bo's incredible books she doesn't expect to find him as recalcitrant as his creations. She has two weeks to make the most of this once in a lifetime opportunity and if she can have a little fun along the way with the hot writer, so be it.

But when she finds herself falling for the hermit, will she be able to walk away?

THE GOOD GUY

Kristen Lewis leads a glamorous life in Singapore as an executive producer of an exciting travel show. She's driven, focussed and never gives in to impulsive decisions, like a one night stand with a sexy stranger.
So imagine her surprise when she's head-hunted for a position at a Melbourne TV studio and discovers her new boss is the guy who rocked her world for that one memorable night.
Nathan Boyd is one of Australia's top entrepreneurs. Throwing himself into work is the only way he knows how to cope with his grief. When he discovers Kris, the first woman to capture his attention in a long time, is now working alongside him, he's thrown.
When Kristen reveals her secret to Nathan, she becomes embroiled in a drama that belongs onscreen rather than off. Will Nate be able to face his fears and take a chance on them?

THE SHY GUY
EXTRACT

Wally the wombat waddled out of his burrow into the sunshine and blinked. He was having a bad day. His friend Mandy the mole had upped and left him after getting married. No, this wouldn't do at all. He had to find a new friend to help him dig all day. Fast.

Bo Bradford's blog, Sunday.

"How cute is that?"

Tahnee Lewis looked up from the computer screen and rolled her eyes at her sister Carissa. "You think that's cute? Wait until you see the pictures I come up with to dazzle the elusive Bo Bradford with."

Carissa smiled and slid into the ergonomic chair next to her. "I have no doubt you'll dazzle this guy and become world famous and probably never speak to me ever again. But what I want to know is does he usually use Wally as a substitute for himself? His blog posts are cute but kind of sad too."

Tahnee shrugged, her gaze drawn back to the screen with its colourful graphics and quirky animal drawings—which, to her critical and purely objective eye, weren't a patch on what she could produce.

"I have no idea. That's why I did an online search and this blog is all I can come up with, along with the requisite social media profiles, but no photos. His website is limited to a backlist of books and a brief bio without a pic."

"Don't most authors have photos on their websites at least? For promotional purposes?"

"Uh-huh, so his reclusiveness makes the elusive Mr. Bradford all the more intriguing."

When starting out in the publishing business, Tahnee would've given her best charcoals to work for a guy like Bo Bradford: Australia's number one children's author, with every book he penned a certifiable winner. His reputation hadn't dimmed in the last five years since he'd been published and though she could hold her own as an illustrator, she knew working with him would guarantee her work for life.

"You're actually going to live with this guy for two weeks?" A small frown creased Carissa's brow, the same frown she wore when her step-daughter Molly got into mischief. "And you know nothing about him?"

"Relax. My publisher put me in touch with his agent who organised the whole thing. Bo's on the up and up. I'll be living in a semi-detached flat attached to his place and this arrangement is going to be a win-win for both of us. He needs a new illustrator, I need a new job. And if all goes well, he'll hire me on a permanent basis."

Boy, did she need a new job. She was so close to achieving her lifelong dream, and having her publisher go under wouldn't deter her. She needed the money now more than ever.

Carissa's frown didn't disappear. "Yeah, but what's with having you live-in? The guy could be some sort of weirdo."

The same thought had crossed Tahnee's mind but the

publishing world was small and she'd asked a few discreet questions, more than satisfied with the answers that the mysterious Bo Bradford was legit.

"He writes children's books." Tahnee rolled her eyes. "Do you see Wally having some kind of strange S&M fetish?"

Carissa's concerned gaze flicked to the PC screen and her frown vanished. "Good point. I guess a guy who spends his days creating cute little critters like Wally the Wombat can't be all bad."

"Exactly. Now, do you want to help me pack or what?"

"Like it's going to take you long to pack ten pairs of jeans, your oldest denim jacket and the few tops you throw on under it."

Tahnee stood and placed a hand on her hip, thrusting out a leg clad in her favourite dark denim. "Are you trying to tell me something about my wardrobe?"

Carissa grinned. "Only the same thing I've been trying to tell you since we were reunited and I could finally give sisterly advice."

"Let me guess. Not all men are attracted to denim?" She waggled her finger under Carissa's nose. "I've got news for you. The guys I date like it just fine."

"Right. And your last date was when?"

Okay, so her know-it-all, disgustingly-happy sister had a point. It had been a while since Tahnee had dated. Ten months to be exact. Not that she was counting or anything.

"All I'm trying to say is you don't know anything about this guy so it mightn't hurt to pack a few extras." Carissa's blue eyes glazed over in that dreamy, romantic haze she usually reserved for talking about her husband Brody, the single dad neighbour who'd taken one look at her sister and turned into a marshmallow. "Who knows? He might expect you to dress up for dinner?"

Tahnee laughed and shook her head. "What century are

you living in? Girl, you've turned into a total sap since you got married."

"Nothing wrong with wanting my sister to be happy," Carissa said, the goofy grin on her face matching the gleam in her eyes.

"You're so right. I'll make sure all the single girls in Stockton know you're on the warpath."

Carissa chuckled. "You always need to have the last word."

"Too right. Now, I have a few hundred pairs of jeans that need folding so want to help?"

Carissa threw a cushion at her and she ducked, knowing she'd miss this even for a fortnight. Discovering her sisters Carissa and Kristen eight years earlier—after they'd been separated as youngsters following the death of their parents and adopted out to different families—had been surreal and getting reacquainted with her sisters had been a blast. Since meeting Carissa they'd been virtually inseparable. Until big, bad Brody came on the scene and her sister turned into a soppy romantic, though thankfully she still saw a lot of Carissa and her adorable kids, Molly and Jack, her six-month bundle of joy.

Family and friends were important to Tahnee, security more so, and she'd do anything to preserve it, including living with an eccentric stranger for two weeks in the hope to secure a stellar reputation in her field for the rest of her career.

Yeah, she could do this.

Two weeks in Sydney would be a breeze and winning over the reclusive Bo Bradford her number one priority.

And if he turned out to be a psycho, she'd stab him with her sharpest pencil.

———

Bo Bradford hated technology.

He hated wasting precious hours on updating his blog daily all in the name of promotion.

He hated telephones breaking his concentration and social media notifications interrupting his thought processes.

And he especially hated the damn intercom signalling the arrival of his replacement illustrator.

He clasped his fingers and stretched forwards to ease the kinks in his neck from staring at the computer too long, then pushed away from his desk and headed for the elaborate intercom system he'd had installed five years earlier when protecting his privacy became all important.

Stabbing at the talk button, he said, "Yes?"

"Tahnee Lewis here, reporting for duty."

Bo reared back from the intercom as if the woman had stuck her finger through it and poked him in the eye. She had a sense of humour? Great. He didn't need a comedienne, he needed a gun illustrator, and though she'd come highly recommended—and he liked what he'd seen of her work for a rival publishing firm—he believed in the old motto 'seeing is believing.'

Hitting the talk button again, he muttered, "Drive through. I'll meet you round the back."

"Right-o. See you in a sec."

Static crackled for several seconds and he realised he hadn't moved, something in the woman's voice captivating his attention. She sounded young. Too young. He needed an expert, not someone to babysit, and the faster he filled Moira's position the better.

Tahnee Lewis also had a tone, a challenging hint of insubordination he didn't like. She made it sound like he'd told her to come in a secret entrance reserved for disreputable folk, when he used the back entrance all the time because it led into the kitchen and family room, the most welcoming and lived in parts of the house.

He shouldn't make snap judgements, but ever since Moira had upped and left him in the lurch—okay, so his quiet illustrator may have had the longest engagement in history and had warned him she'd be out of here once the wedding ring slipped on her finger—he'd been floundering.

He had a deadline to meet and a position to fill and he placed a lot of faith in Tahnee Lewis. She better be worth it.

A funny knock reminiscent of the beat of an old eighties tune came from the kitchen door and he quickly saved the document he'd been working on and headed out the back.

He was big on first impressions, always had been, and the minute he opened the door he knew he was in trouble.

"Bo Bradford? I'm Tahnee Lewis, pleased to meet you."

Bo shook her hand automatically, trying not to stare at the tall, stunning blonde standing on his doorstep, and failing miserably.

He'd expected a professionally dressed woman with an equally business-like demeanour.

What he got was a denim-clad teeny bopper with challenge in her deep blue eyes and a cheeky quirk to her full lips.

This woman didn't look like the subservient type used to taking orders from a grumpy author subject to creative whims. No way.

With the face of a naughty devil and the body of an angel, she looked like one thing to him.

Trouble.

"Did I catch you at a bad time?"

Bo silently cursed his ineptitude, dropped her hand quickly and stepped aside. "No, come in. I was in the middle of a scene and I tend to get a bit distracted."

"I know exactly what you mean. I do the same thing. Once, I was so in the zone with a sketch that the toaster had a tussle with a piece of bread resulting in smoke filling the kitchen and I didn't even notice."

She smiled and his heart sank.

Her face lit up with a million-dollar smile that could sell toothpaste to dentists. Combined with the sparkling blue eyes, lush mouth, and long blonde hair cut into layers that framed her heart-shaped face, Bo knew she might prove to be more of a distraction than any chapter in his current work in progress.

"Do you need a hand with any more bags?" He pointed to a small wheelie suitcase and a backpack, expecting another bag or ten in the car. The women he'd dated in the past had always needed at least five bags or cases of different sizes to house monster wardrobes. Yet another reason why he preferred living on his own.

"No, this is it."

He tried to mask his shock but must've failed by the twitching corners of her mouth.

That mouth...his gaze flicked past it, desperately trying to stay focused on her eyes. However, the harder he fought, the more tempting it became until he let his gaze dip a fraction, absorbing the shape of her lips, their fullness, their gloss.

"Bo?"

He wondered if living the life of a recluse was a good idea if he started noticing trivial things like his new illustrator's mouth. He didn't have time for dating; women were a distraction he could do without. His work was all-important and finishing this next book on time vital.

"Yeah?"

"I'd kill for a coffee," she said, sending a pointed glance at the espresso machine on the bench behind him. "If you don't mind, that is."

"No problem. How do you like it?"

For one long, loaded moment their gazes locked, her lips

parted a fraction, and he could've sworn the air sizzled with static electricity as if they'd just been through a freak storm.

How do you like it? He hadn't meant it as a come-on, far from it, and he didn't like the way she stared at him with those knowing blue eyes, as if assessing him while he grabbed two mugs out of the cupboard and all but slammed them on the granite bench top.

"I like it strong. Hot. Sweet."

Wishing she'd stop staring at him like he'd morphed into Wally's long lost brother and had sprouted ears and fur, he turned his back on her and busied himself with the coffee, hoping this wasn't a mistake. He had a relentless work ethic and a low tolerance for incompetence and though Tahnee came highly recommended, he didn't like the easy familiarity she'd already slipped into around him: her confident smile, her teasing eyes, and the unshakeable feeling she was laughing at him for being a workaholic author who didn't get out much.

"How many sugars?"

"Two, please. No milk."

He heard a rustling and crackle of paper bags being opened and he hoped she wasn't pulling out any more surprises. He'd had enough in the last few minutes to last him a while.

Moira had been the perfect co-worker: reserved, dependable, and a non-distraction with her light brown hair, no make-up and navy business suits. He'd never had the impulse to study Moira's mouth.

He'd been one hundred percent focussed on work around Moira and they'd been a cohesive team. With Tahnee, he had an awful suspicion that associating teamwork with the gorgeous blonde might lead him to ponder other creative directions altogether, directions he hadn't headed down in a long while, directions that had nothing to do with words or pictures or kids stories.

"Can I tempt you?"

Bo almost jumped out of his skin as she snuck up behind him and offered an open paper bag filled with plump croissants, the mouth-watering buttery aroma combining with a fresh, floral scent he'd inhaled earlier as she'd walked into the room.

"Thanks," he muttered, taking a croissant and turning back to pouring the coffee.

His reaction to her was insane, stupid and counter-productive. He needed Tahnee Lewis to finish his book; he didn't need her distracting him with an amused expression permanently etched on her beautiful face.

Sighing in resignation, he turned back to find her staring at him with a smug smile as if she knew exactly how annoyed he was and was enjoying every minute.

The woman was a nuisance.

The woman was a curse.

The woman had to save his butt so for now, she'd stay.

―――

Tahnee sipped at her coffee and tried not to stare at her new boss.

Tried and failed.

Little wonder Bo Bradford didn't have a pic on his website. The number of hits he'd get would send the internet into meltdown.

She watched him fuss around the kitchen looking for a plate to dump the croissants on—Carissa's favourite almond custard croissants her sister had thrust into her hand for the two hour drive to Sydney. Tahnee hadn't felt like eating on the drive down. Lucky for her, considering Bo looked like he could do with a bit of sweetening up. He may be the hottest guy on the eastern seaboard of Australia but boy, did he need to lighten up.

"These smell good," he said, placing the plate between them and sliding into a seat opposite her as he glanced at the logo on the paper bag. "*Michelle's*? Never heard of it."

"It's a small bakery in Stockton, where I live."

Where I'll always live, she refrained from adding. She belonged in Stockton; she liked the comfort of knowing every one in town, she liked the cosy atmosphere and best of all, she'd never felt as secure as she did there, a feeling she'd do anything to preserve.

"It won't be a problem you staying here for a few weeks?"

She bit back a smile. What Mr. Nosy was really asking was if she had any ties to Stockton, namely a significant other.

Fine, her boss was entitled to know stuff like that, but with her vivid imagination—and her appreciation for a fine looking guy--she almost wished there was more than a professional interest.

Yeah, right, like her grumpy boss would be looking for a fling while trialling her for the most important job of her career. Get real.

"No problem at all. I have an overprotective sister back home who quizzed me at length about staying here, and another sister who's overseas, working in Singapore, but apart from that I'm footloose and fancy-free."

Tahnee mentally clapped a hand over her mouth. Why did she say that? Guys who looked like him would probably take it as a come-on. She needed to smarten up her act or she'd be out on her butt along with her sketchbook and charcoals.

He stared at her over the rim of his coffee mug, his steady, green gaze unwavering. "Good. We don't have time for distractions. I need to get my current book done ASAP."

"Tight deadline?"

His eyes froze, the peculiar green-blue hue the exact colour of an icy glacier she'd seen on an Alaskan documentary once. "Exactly," he said, his flat tone matching his frigid eyes. "If you've finished your coffee, I'll show you the flat."

O-kay. Was it something she said?

The guy was prickly. Extremely sexy, but very prickly, and she hated having to tread on eggshells. She'd never been that type of person, preferring blunt honesty to games—which probably explained why she was eternally single and couldn't hold onto a guy beyond a few dates.

A shame, considering she wouldn't mind the whole hubby-two point five kids—white picket fence-dream one day. After all, how much more secure could she get when surrounded by a family she created?

After finishing her coffee in three quick gulps, she stood and headed for the sink to rinse her mug. "I'm ready."

Anything to diffuse the weird tension that had enveloped them; the atmosphere seemed taut since she'd arrived and when she'd asked him about his book he'd gone cold on her. Just what she needed, a temperamental artist to work with.

She turned and caught him staring at her butt before he quickly raised his gaze to eye level and she smothered a giggle. Bo blew hotter and colder than a Melbourne day. First, he froze her out, now he looked decidedly flustered. Cute, considering he had everything she valued in a guy: great pecs and flat abs hugged by a grey T-shirt, lean legs moulded by faded denim, just over six foot, amazing eyes, short back and sides, facial features arranged just right.

Okay, so she was trying to play down the high cheekbones, straight nose, clean jaw and overall symmetry of his face but hey, she needed to concentrate on work, not her boss's model potential.

"Come on, let's go. I haven't got all day," he muttered, a frown marring his brow.

This time, Tahnee couldn't stifle her smile at his barked

order and as she followed him, letting him carry her bags for being such a grump, she did a bit of butt-checking of her own, not surprised it matched the rest of his perfection.

Hmm...maybe finding inspiration for her work over the next two weeks wouldn't be so difficult after all.

READ THE SHY GUY.

FREE BOOK AND MORE

SIGN UP TO NICOLA'S NEWSLETTER for a free book!

Read Nicola's feel-good romance **DID NOT FINISH**

Or her gothic suspense novels **THE RETREAT** and **THE HAVEN**

(The gothic prequel **THE RESIDENCE** is free!)

Try the **CARTWRIGHT BROTHERS** duo

FASCINATION

PERFECTION

The **WORKPLACE LIAISONS** duo

THE BOSS

THE CEO

The **REDEEMING A BAD BOY** series

THE REBEL

THE PLAYER

THE WANDERER

THE CHARMER

THE EX (releasing September 2024)

THE FRIEND (releasing October 2024

Try the **BASHFUL BRIDES** series

NOT THE MARRYING KIND

NOT THE ROMANTIC KIND

NOT THE DARING KIND

NOT THE DATING KIND

The **CREATIVE IN LOVE** series

THE GRUMPY GUY

THE SHY GUY

THE GOOD GUY

Try the **BOMBSHELLS** series

BEFORE (FREE!)

BRASH

BLUSH

BOLD

BAD

BOMBSHELLS BOXED SET

The **WORLD APART** series

WALKING THE LINE (FREE!)

CROSSING THE LINE

TOWING THE LINE

BLURRING THE LINE

WORLD APART BOXED SET

The **HOT ISLAND NIGHTS** duo

WICKED NIGHTS

WANTON NIGHTS

The **ROMANCE CYNICS** duo

CUPID SEASON

SORRY SEASON

The **BOLLYWOOD BILLIONAIRES** series

FAKING IT

MAKING IT

The **LOOKING FOR LOVE** series

LUCKY LOVE

CRAZY LOVE

SAPPHIRES ARE A GUY'S BEST FRIEND

THE SECOND CHANCE GUY

Check out Nicola's website for a full list of her books.

And read her other romances as Nikki North.

'MILLIONAIRE IN THE CITY' series.

LUCKY

FANCY

FLIRTY

FOLLY

MADLY

Check out the **ESCAPE WITH ME** series.
TRUST ME
FORGIVE ME

Try the **LAW BREAKER** series
THE DEAL MAKER
THE CONTRACT BREAKER

About the Author

USA TODAY bestselling and multi-award winning author Nicola Marsh writes page-turning fiction to keep you up all night.
She's published 86 books and sold millions of copies worldwide.
She currently writes contemporary romance and domestic suspense.
She's also a Waldenbooks, Bookscan, Amazon, iBooks and Barnes & Noble bestseller, a RBY (Romantic Book of the Year) and National Readers' Choice Award winner, and a multi-finalist for a number of awards including the Romantic Times Reviewers' Choice Award, HOLT Medallion, Booksellers' Best, Golden Quill, Laurel Wreath, and More than Magic.
A physiotherapist for thirteen years, she now adores writing full time, raising her two dashing young heroes, sharing fine food with family and friends, and her favorite, curling up with a good book!

Printed in Great Britain
by Amazon